The Holy Family, by Pieter van Avont, in a garland of fruit, flowers and vegetables painted by Jan Bruegel the Elder. Early seventeenth century

REAY TANNAHILL

The Fine Art of Food

SOUTH BRUNSWICK AND NEW YORK:
A. S. BARNES AND COMPANY

© The Folio Society Ltd 1968

First American Edition 1970

Published by
A. S. Barnes & Co., Inc.
Cranbury, N. J. 08512

Library of Congress
Catalogue Card Number: 70-118672

ISBN 0-498-07713-6

Printed and bound in Great Britain
by Jarrold and Sons Ltd, Norwich
Set in 12 point Garamond 2 points leaded

Preface

A comprehensive history of food through the ages would occupy many more, and thicker, volumes than the present one. The subject is so basic that its influences can be traced on almost every level of human activity. What men eat and drink is shaped not only by cooking techniques and equipment, but by agriculture and animal husbandry, by the availability of water and fuel, by knowledge of botany, biology, and the ecology of plants, insects and animals. Success or failure in the quest for food has dictated population growth and urban development, as well as economic, social and political theory. And the quest itself has been the catalyst of exploration, trade, technological development, and—not infrequently—war and dominion.

In *The Fine Art of Food* it has been possible to touch on very few of these subjects, but instead of restricting the book to a description of how the various national cuisines have developed over the centuries, I have chosen to give a general picture of what people ate during various periods, and in what form they ate it. I have tried, also, to show how the logic of the kitchen often produced the same answers in countries separated by thousands of miles or thousands of years—how, for example, the Indian *chapati* is related to the Scots oatcake, and the modern American clambake to the food of prehistoric man. I have stressed, too, the ramifications of trade, and how Europe absorbed into its diet all the foods that the rest of the world could offer: tea from China, sugar, spices, and the domestic fowl from India, coffee from the Levant, potatoes from Peru, maize and chocolate from Central America, fruits and vegetables from many other lands. Because the book has been constructed in these terms, such famous names as Lucullus, Epicurus and—to leap the centuries—Brillat-Savarin, are missing; quite simply, they would have been irrelevant.

The 'fine art' of the title relates, not to culinary genius, but to the illustrations, which have been chosen partly to amplify the text and partly to show how painters have looked at food in the context of their own times. The temptation to include a large proportion of 'still lives' was great but had to be resisted; the pictures are intended to provide historical documentation as well as visual pleasure.

The book is divided in a roughly chronological sequence as follows: there is first a chapter on prehistory, Sumer and Egypt; this is followed by Greece and Rome, then by a short chapter on Europe in the so-called 'Dark Ages' (c. AD 400–1100). India and China, which provided the spices so necessary to the European diet for many centuries, come next, then Europe in the Middle Ages, the Renaissance, and after (*c.* 1100–1650). Then there is a chapter on the newly discovered Americas, and the main part of the book ends with Europe from around 1650 until 1900. Finally, there is a brief epilogue dealing with food in art through the ages.

There are many short quotations in the book, translated from various languages. In the case of mediaeval English, I have modernized the words while leaving the original sentence structure; most of the quotations are integrated into the text, and I see no reason why the reader should lose the thread of the narrative by having to struggle with Chaucerian spelling. The sources of all quotations are given at the end of the book. They are not numbered in the text; instead, the list of sources gives the page number and a key word or words which should enable the reader to identify any particular quotation without difficulty.

The publishers and I would like to thank the many galleries, museums and photographers who have provided illustrations and, in some cases, helped us trace pictures of whose locations we were uncertain. All are credited in the list of illustrations on page 125.

One

'I am convinced', said Sydney Smith, 'that character, talents, virtues, and qualities are powerfully affected by beef, mutton, pie crust, and rich soups.'

It was not a new idea. Greek physicians had built an entire system of dietetics on it two thousand years earlier. And centuries before that, men had recognized that food nourished not only the body, but the mind. 'Food is better than power', advised the Indian *Upanishads* in the eighth century BC. 'If a man abstain from food for ten days, though he live, he would not be able to see, hear, perceive, think, act, and understand. But when he obtains food, he is able to see, hear, perceive, think, act, and understand.'

When he obtains food . . . It is a phrase with the widest implications, because the history of food is inextricably linked with the history of mankind. In the last analysis, without food there would *be* no history—and no mankind.

The earth has been inhabited for millions of years, but modern knowledge of the past covers only the last six thousand of them, and much of that inadequately. For the period prior to 1500 BC, the most overworked words in the historian's vocabulary are 'perhaps . . . probably . . . it seems likely'.

It is generally accepted that primitive man was a hunter. He tracked down

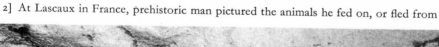

2] At Lascaux in France, prehistoric man pictured the animals he fed on, or fled from

his food, killed it, and ate it uncooked and unseasoned. At first, he knew no way of preserving it, but eventually discovered that cooked meat lasted longer than raw. It may have taken tens of thousands of years for this technique to become general. Roast meat probably tasted very odd to men accustomed to raw, and they would certainly find it indigestible. Nor would boiled meat be any more appetizing. Before cooking-pots were invented, water was placed in a hollow of rock, or in a bag made from the hide of the slaughtered animal, and heated by dropping in fire-warmed stones. It must have been a slow process, during which a great deal of the flavour seeped out of the meat into the water. We have no way of knowing whether primitive man drank the broth or merely tossed it away.

Man's next discovery was that it was possible, instead of killing animals, to keep them in captivity. Man the hunter became man the herdsman. Soon, too, he became a cultivator, when he found that seeds could be made to grow where he willed. The seeds of certain grasses provided a pleasant seasoning for his food, and he set about cultivating them—particularly those varieties in which the seed clung firmly to the stalk and resisted the wind. In the course of thousands of years, what had originally been wild grasses became the millet, the oats, the barley and the wheat of civilized man.

Information on food in prehistoric times is scanty. By 5000 BC, there were goats, pigs, sheep, oxen and cows in Egypt. Pig bones have been found in kitchen refuse heaps dating from Neolithic times. In France, Victorian archaeologists dug up the skeletons of a hundred thousand horses, relics of the menu favoured by prehistoric man in Burgundy. Even allowing for the fact that the horse was then no larger than a very small pony, this suggests a thriving human society established over an appreciable period. In South America, Stone Age man lived off mammoth steaks, as well as smaller animals, fruits, nuts and grain. And in North America, mortars and grinding-stones have been unearthed near dried up lakes in California and Texas—which implies that Stone Age North Americans ground nuts and seeds into flour to use with their caribou and bison meat, their fruit and edible roots. Along the California seaboard, seafood was probably also part of the staple diet.

By deduction and—in some cases—by radio-carbon dating, it can be said that early man knew how to preserve meat by cooking, that he had discovered how to cultivate certain plants, that he attributed medicinal properties to certain herbs, that (probably by mistake) he had discovered the process of fermentation and the virtues and vices of primitive wine and beer, and that he had invented cooking-pots. So much, and not much more.

Then, suddenly, history begins. Deduction gives way to the written, if fragmentary, records of an established civilization, that of Sumer *c.* 3500 BC. Sumer did not, like the dragon's teeth, spring fully armed from the soil. The Sumerians themselves were wanderers who arrived in southern Iraq and found there an already established society. But, in the country better known by its later name of Babylon, they developed an urban civilization and committed many of its laws and legends to clay tablets which have survived and been deciphered.

These tablets record the existence of many foods still known today. The Sumerian temples, for example, had their tributary lands and draught-cattle —as religious institutions have had throughout history—and one ancient inscription (*c.* 2400 BC) complained that civic dignitaries were guilty of misappropriating temple funds. 'The oxen of the gods ploughed the *ensi*'s [city governor's] onion patches; the onion and cucumber patches of the *ensi* were located in the gods' best fields.'

There was garlic as well as onions, and chick-peas, plants of the bean family, lentils, turnips, lettuce, cress, leeks and mustard. Among the ingredients required for remedies listed on a medical tablet (*c.* 2750 BC) were thyme, pears and figs. The dry ingredients were to be pulverized, says one prescription, and made into a thick paste. Then 'pour beer over it, rub with oil, fasten as a poultice'.

Educated Sumerians had literary tastes, and one of the works still extant hints at the richness of the countryside during a period of prosperity. It is a *Dispute between Emesh* [summer] *and Enten* [winter]:

> Enten made the ewe give birth to the lamb, the goat give birth to the kid,
> Cow and calf to multiply, fat and milk to increase,
> In the plain he made rejoice the heart of the wild goat, sheep and donkey,
> The birds of heaven—in the wide earth he made them set up their nests,
> The fish of the sea—in the canebreak he made them lay their eggs,
> In the [date-] palm grove and vineyard he made honey and wine abound,
> The trees, wherever planted, he caused to bear fruit,
> The gardens he decked out in green, made their plants luxuriant,
> Made grain increase in the furrows,
> Like Ashnan [the grain goddess], the kindly maid, he made it come
> forth sturdily.

As the *Dispute* relates, there were sheep, goats and cows, as well as draught-oxen in Sumer. That ancient scavenger, the pig—descendant of the wild hog —also roamed the streets of the city-states, thriving on fodder that would have sustained no other domesticated animal but the goose. (In spite of their shrill natures, the pig and the goose have been favoured through the centuries for their knack of surviving on the scantiest diet.) Sumerians hunted the deer, the gazelle and the wild boar, while trappers snared birds, and fishermen caught fifty recorded species of fish.

Sumerian agriculture was advanced and systematic, and the irrigation system was highly developed. Since constant irrigation tends to increase the chemical salt content of the soil, the main crop was barley, which is better able to withstand these conditions than wheat. Sesame was another major crop, important for its oil.

3] Goats, sheep and cattle in Sumer, *c.* 2500 B C

Agricultural labourers must have been many and hard-working, and in all probability their diet was no more varied than the diet of labourers has ever been—the barley cakes, onions and beer of Sumer 3000 B C have their parallel in the bread, cheese and beer of nineteenth-century England. The better-off members of the community, however, must have led quite comfortable lives, frequently dining off meat, fish or poultry (excluding chicken, which was not introduced from India until after Sumer had vanished), roasted, or boiled with vegetables or barley into a dish which was half stew, half porridge. There were barley cakes and fruit and, in the kitchen, large clay or stone jars of beer and clarified butter.

4] *Above:* cutting corn, and threshing grain by driving cattle over it
Below: ploughing, necessary when the Nile waters did not flood to their full extent

Just as man cannot exist without food, settled communities cannot exist without water. Sumer flourished on the Euphrates and, at much the same time, six hundred miles to the west, Egypt drew life and prosperity from the Nile. 'In that country', said Pliny, 'the Nile plays the part of farmer, beginning to overflow its banks at the new moon in midsummer, at first gently and then more violently, as long as the sun is in the constellation of the Lion. Then when the sun has passed over into the Virgin it slows down, and when the sun is in the Scales it subsides. . . . [It used to be the custom] to begin sowing after the subsidence of the Nile and then to drive swine over the ground, pressing down the seed in the damp soil with their feet, and I believe that in former days this was the common practice, and that at the present day also the sowing is done without much heavier labour.' When the Nile waters overflowed and retreated, they left behind them black earth deposits, rich in minerals, from the Ethiopian plateau. All that was needed was to scatter seed on the mud and drive sheep or pigs over the land to settle it. 'When the Nile overflows the land', says an Egyptian papyrus of 1300 BC, 'then has the servant no need to plough. Everybody snores.'

The Egyptians made use of every inch of rich land in the Nile valley. Wheat was the basis of the economy of the Pharaohs, and it was wheat that enabled the Egyptians to discover raised bread. Formerly, bread had consisted of grain flour mixed with water and possibly a few flavouring ingredients, shaped into a flat cake, and baked on a hot stone until crisp on the outside. One day, presumably, the wind wafted some yeast spores on to a wheaten dough mix— and leavening was discovered. Unaware of the precise nature of the leavening agent, the Egyptians carefully preserved a fragment of each day's dough to implant the raising agent in the next day's bread. Wheat was the key to their success, for raised bread is not made satisfactorily with millet, oats or barley —which cannot properly retain the gases produced by leavening—and rye, which can, had not yet been cultivated.

Within a short time, the ancient Egyptians were producing as many varieties of bread as we can boast today. They added poppy seeds, sesame or camphor; mixed the dough with honey, butter, milk or eggs; made oval loaves, round ones, conical or plaited ones. The usual bread was called *ta*, and it was made at home, being baked in pottery dishes heated over the fire. The bread oven was introduced *c.* 1500 BC. On great estates there were full-scale bakeries. 'Number of breads' became a measure of wealth, and for hundreds of years wages were paid in bread and beer. A peasant might be paid three breads and two jugs of beer daily, while an important official would receive an annual salary of nine hundred fine wheat breads, thirty-six thousand flat breads, and 360 jugs of beer.

Beer was the national drink of ancient Egypt. It was made from lightly baked barley dough, which was soaked in date-sweetened water until it fermented. The strained-off liquid compared favourably, it was claimed, with good wine. Athenaeus—an Egyptian by birth, who wrote a massive and learned work on food in the third century AD—said that 'Dion, the academic philosopher', reported that 'those who drank this beer were so pleased with it that they sang and danced, and did everything like men drunk with wine. Now Aristotle says that men who are drunk with wine show it in their faces; but that those who have drunk too much beer fall back and go to sleep; for wine is stimulating, but beer has a tendency to stupefy.' Certainly, drunkenness was not unknown in ancient Egypt. There are various surviving papyri concerning manners, and one of them at least recommends: 'Do not get drunk in the taverns in which they drink beer, for fear that people repeat words which may have gone out of thy mouth, without thou having perception of having uttered them.' The Pharaohs might, perhaps, have been wise to follow the example of the rulers of China who, in 1700 BC, forbade intoxicating liquor to all except the aged. Many centuries later, too, the Aztecs of Mexico were to regard immoderate drinking as a crime. The *Codex Mendoza* recorded that 'intoxication was forbidden upon pain of death . . . to men and women alike, yet those who had reached the age of seventy years, provided they had children and grandchildren, were exempt from this prohibition'.

The poor peasant in Egypt consumed great quantities of bread, beer and onions, and probably milk and meat as well—though not every day. Even the rich were slightly restricted in their meat diet, since meat deteriorates very rapidly in a hot climate. Bulls, sheep, goats and pig would be killed only on feast days, or when guests were expected. But geese, duck and pigeons were caged and fattened for the table. So, too, were teal, pintail, widgeon and crane. The Nile marshes contained eel, mullet, carp, perch and tigerfish, but since most fish had, to the Egyptians, some attributes of divinity, there were many taboos involved in treating them as food. Kings and temple officials—'the virtuous ones'—were not permitted to eat fish. Nor, at certain periods, were they permitted to eat mutton. And the milch cow was venerated as much in Egypt, particularly during the later dynasties, as it was in India.

The Egyptians were an enterprising people. They exported cereals and flax. They raised large herds of African cattle and bred several different strains. For centuries, they persisted in attempts to domesticate a number of wild animals. They knew how to dry and salt fish. They extracted as much corn from the Nile valley as modern methods can do today. From pockets of land not devoted to wheat, barley and flax, they provided their tables with gourds, lentils, chick peas, cucumber, onions, leeks and garlic, as well as the mustard seed which they liked to chew with their meat. Wild celery was free for the gathering. Fruit, too, was to be had—figs, grapes, dates, melons and pomegranates. So sweet-toothed were the Egyptians that they could not produce enough honey for their needs (sugar had not as yet been introduced), and had to import extra supplies from Greece and Syria.

When a rich Egyptian sat down to dine, the servants brought in to him a circular table set on a single leg. On the table were loaves of bread and rolls sprinkled with sesame or caraway seeds. There were dishes of boiled or roasted meat (roast goose being a universal favourite) as well as fish which had been dressed, perhaps, with an early version of *tartare* sauce made from the juice of sour grapes. Vegetables were usually served, too—onions are frequently and recognizably represented in ancient tomb paintings—and fruit ended the meal. When there were invited guests, the host and hostess sat together at the head of the room; male guests were seated along one side of the room, women along the other; travellers, strangers and the uninvited were expected to stand. The only dining implements appear to have been fingers and spoons.

5] Geese destined to be caged and fattened for the table

The ancient Egyptians were very conscious of diet, and believed that digestive troubles were the source of most illnesses. As a result, they fasted frequently and dosed themselves with emetics. They were inordinately fond of beer, date wine and grape wine, and had their own methods of averting the effects of indulgence. 'They are', Athenaeus remarks, 'the only people among whom it is a custom at their feasts to eat boiled cabbages before all the rest of their food.' It was a custom endorsed by the great botanist, Theophrastus, who said that 'the vine as long as it lives always turns away from the smell of cabbage'!

Grape wine was a prerogative of the rich Egyptian. The vine had been imported from Asia and flourished in Egypt from about 3000 BC, being used initially to provide funerary wines. But important people soon began to cultivate it for table wine, which was usually white and often very fine. Some wines were reputedly left to mature for two hundred years in tall sealed amphorae, neatly labelled with the year, the type, the name of the vineyard and of the owner. The yield was high in many areas, for the grapes ripened all the year round, but the finest wines came from the oases and parts of the Nile delta. According to Athenaeus, the wine known as Mareotic—which was produced near Alexandria—was 'white and sweet and good for the breath and digestible'. For several centuries, Egyptian wine had an international reputation, but as the country was gradually impoverished by the exploitation of the Roman emperors, production diminished. When, in the seventh century AD, the Arabs swept into Egypt under the banner of Islam, viticulture ended. Wine, the Prophet had said, was 'an abomination', and throughout the lands of the Caliphates it virtually disappeared.

Two

While Babylon expanded the heritage of Sumer, while Egypt flourished, other civilizations began to burgeon. In India, from *c*. 2500 BC until *c*. 1500 BC, the Indus valley civilization reached a high stage of development; wheat and barley were grown, many animals domesticated; there were ovens for bread, and grinding-stones for spices. In China, wheat and millet were grown during the third millennium BC, and by 2000 BC a thriving trade had developed in several products, notably salt. In western Asia, Persia was approaching its period of magnificence. And in the Mediterranean that great seafaring race, the Phoenicians, established a network of trading stations and supplied wines to Greece, vines to Spain, and Eastern spices to all the ports of southern Europe. They were the merchant princes and middlemen of the ancient world.

Some time before 1000 BC, groups of barbarian nomads began to drift south from the forests of central and eastern Europe towards the warmer lands of the Mediterranean. Some of these nomads settled around the Aegean. Others colonized the Italian peninsula. They were the founding fathers of two civilizations which have gripped the world's imagination ever since—'classical' Greece and Rome.

In the early days, the Greeks were not really an agricultural people. To them, heads of cattle were a greater index of wealth than fields of corn. This may have been partly due to their nomadic ancestry, for cattle can be kept on the move while fields of corn cannot. Furthermore, the soil of Greece was poor and shallow and much of the land mountainous. But the olive and the vine flourished, so the Greeks chose to grow what barley they could and to import their wheat requirements from Sicily, Egypt or the Black Sea. (It has been argued, quite persuasively, that the legend of Jason and the Argonauts is simply the record of a grain expedition to the Black Sea, Jason being the overseer in charge of the venture, and the Golden Fleece the grain which was to be taken back home.)

Barley-meal, olives, wine, fish as a relish, and meat on high days and holidays—this was the basic diet of the ancient Greeks, though the farmer-poet Hesiod paints a much more appealing picture in his *Works and Days* (on which Virgil later modelled the *Georgics*). Contemplating the heat of summer, Hesiod says:

> Then in a great rock's shadow, with milk-bread, let me lie,
> And Byblian wine, and milk from goats just going dry,
> And flesh of an uncalved heifer, fed in a forest glade,
> Or kids first-born of their mother. So let me sit in the shade,
> With a bellyful within me, sipping at my ease
> The fire-red wine, and turning to face the western breeze.

Hesiod's 'Byblian wine' was an import from Byblos in Phoenicia, and was probably fragrant and sweet to the tongue. The heroes of Greek legend, however—if Homer is to be believed—were more inclined to favour the home product, Pramnian wine. This, thanks to Homer, has become one of the most famous wines of antiquity, although Aristophanes maintained that it was a great deal too harsh for Athenian tastes. Like most wines of the classical world, Pramnian was drunk mixed rather than neat. When, in the *Iliad*, the lady Hecamede served wine to Nestor and Machaon, she first placed a handsome table before them. 'On this she put a bronze dish, an onion to eat as a relish with the drink, some yellow honey, and sacred barley-meal; and beside these a magnificent beaker adorned with golden studs. . . . In this cup, their comely attendant mixed them the pottage with Pramnian wine, and after making it ready by grating into it some goat's milk cheese with a bronze grater and sprinkling white barley on top, she invited them to drink, which they did.'

The heroes of the *Iliad* had hearty appetites for roast meat, plain and simple and appetizing. 'Patroclus . . . put down a big bench in the firelight, and laid on it the backs of a sheep and a fat goat and the chine of a great hog rich in lard. Automedon held these for him, while Achilles jointed them, and then carved up the joints and spitted the slices. Meanwhile, Patroclus, the royal son of Menoetius, made the fire blaze up. When it had burnt down again and the flames had disappeared, he scattered the embers and laid the spits above them, resting them on dogs, after he had sprinkled the meat with holy salt. When he had roasted it and heaped it up on platters, Patroclus fetched some bread and set it out on the table in handsome baskets; and Achilles divided the meat into portions.' The epic splendour of the Greek heroes would have been sadly diminished if they had fed, instead, on the dormice in vineleaves and dainty cheesecakes of imperial Rome.

Greek cooking was not, in the early days, particularly refined. This was natural enough, since what we call 'Greece' was in fact a collection of small states, only loosely linked together, most of whose inhabitants were of the countryside rather than the city. Even in the cities, the Greeks were much inclined to spend their leisure time—which was considerable, since they rose at dawn and worked to live rather than to live-in-luxury—out of doors. And a simple and basic diet, without frills, is characteristic of almost all outdoor societies in all ages. Yet though the average Greek was no great gourmet, even he shuddered at the diet favoured by the earnest and austere Spartans, whose black broth—reputedly made of pork stock, vinegar and salt—was infamous throughout the civilized world. Indeed, Athenaeus reports that 'a citizen of Sybaris, who was staying at Sparta, and who dined in their public mess-hall, said: "It is natural enough for the Spartans to be the bravest of men; for any man in his senses would rather die ten thousand times over than live as miserably as this."'

In the middle of the fifth century BC, however, the situation began to change. It was the time of Pericles and the building of the Parthenon; of Herodotus, Aeschylus, Sophocles and Euripides. Athens became a centre of magnificence and learning, rich and self-assured. It would have been strange indeed if this new sophistication had not struck an echo in the Athenian kitchen. No ancient Greek cookery books remain, but several were certainly written. Authors such as Glaucus the Locrian, Mithaecus, Heraclidus, Agis, Hegesippus, Eristratus and Euthydemus wrote treatises more or less directly related to food, with titles such as *On Cookery*, *Gastronomy*, *On Pickles*, *On Vegetables* and *Sicilian Cookery* (Sicily was then one of the most populous states of Greater Greece). The father of all Greek cookery-writers and, according to his own assertion, the inventor of 'made' dishes, was Archestratus who, in the fourth century BC, quartered the known world in search of information on food and drink.

As time went on, Athens found herself importing pepper, sesame oil and rice from faraway India, and became largely dependent on imports for her grain supplies. These imports were paid for out of the profits from exported wine and olive oil. Attic oil was generally agreed to be the finest in the world, and the olive also provided lamp oil and the ancient equivalent of soap.

Some idea of the variety of foods known in the later period of classical

6] A Greek banquet scene in the sixth century B C

Greece can be gathered from Teleclides' *Amphictyons*, in which the author envisaged the pleasures of paradise. 'The streams all ran with rosy wine, and barley cakes fought with wheaten loaves to be the first to reach a hungry man's open mouth. . . . Fish too came straight to men's doors and fried themselves, all ready, dished themselves up, and stood upon the table before the guests. A stream of soup flowed along in front of all the couches, bearing with it chunks of smoking-hot meat. And rivulets of white sauce brought, to all who chose to eat, the sweetest forcemeat balls. So that there was no lack, but all ate what they wanted. Dishes there were of boiled meat, too, and sausages and pasties. And roasted thrushes and rissoles flew down men's throats as if spontaneously. There were the sounds, too, of cheesecakes champed in men's hungry jaws, while the youngsters toyed with pieces of tripe and paunch and liver.' Fruit and vegetables were apparently not regarded as essential to paradise, although the Greeks certainly ate pears, pomegranates, figs, apples and medlars, and seem to have numbered among their vegetables onions, gourds, mushrooms, asparagus, cucumber, lettuce and cauliflower.

It has been suggested that the Greek cuisine achieved a state of Enlightenment after Alexander the Great's expeditions to Egypt, Persia, Babylon and

India. The returning Greek soldier, it is said, brought back with him a taste for the spices and delicacies of the East. This is not necessarily true. He may, in fact, have been only too delighted to get back to home cooking, to see the end of the strange foods which were all that foreign lands could supply. Or he may have enjoyed them when he was abroad, but given them up without regret when he returned home—if he ever did, for it was a long and hazardous journey back from the valley of the Indus. The most that can be said is that returning soldiers were probably familiar with the delicacies of the East. And since (on all but the most sophisticated levels of society) unfamiliarity is the major barrier to acceptance of new foods, any enterprising merchant who later imported such delicacies stood a better chance of selling them than he would have done under other circumstances.

At a civilized Greek meal, said Archestratus:

> Round a table delicately spread,
> Or three, or four, may sit in choice repast,
> Or five at most.

More than that, he argued, changed dinner into Bedlam. When Rome achieved greatness, her citizens were inclined to agree with him, although they favoured increasing the number slightly, to eight or nine at most. If this seems a very inadequate number for an orgy—and, to many people, the word 'orgy' follows 'Rome' as night follows day—it should be remembered that, in addition to guests, there were frequently several hangers-on (more correctly known as 'parasites'), as well as entertainers, unservile slaves, and, after dinner, ladies of the town.

Roman diners were accommodated on couches arranged in a 'U' shape and called the *triclinium*. When the guests were seated, their slippers were removed. If the host was rich or pretentious, his guests might then be subjected to a full-scale pedicure, although it was more usual for slaves simply to bring round ewers of water so that they might wash their hands and bathe the dust of the street from their feet. The table was set in the centre of the 'U' and, as the courses came and went, 'a high-girt slave with purple napkin wiped well the maple-wood table, while a second swept up the scraps and anything that could offend the guests'. This last, slightly sinister phrase (from one of Horace's *Satires*) takes on meaning when it is realized that Roman wall hangings and canopies occasionally came adrift, descending 'in mighty ruin upon the platter, trailing more black dust than the north wind raises on Campanian plains'. When this happened, guests were inclined to call for their slippers—a sign that they intended instant departure.

What did the Romans eat? It would be easier to say what they did *not* eat, for in the great days of imperial Rome there was very little that did not appear on the tables of the rich. There were no tomatoes, no potatoes, no pineapples, no maize, probably no rye, and certainly no turkey. Tea, coffee and chocolate were unknown. Useful animals such as the ox, the cow and the horse were never slaughtered for food. The Romans did not drink cow's milk or use butter or cream in cooking, although they did import butter from Narbonne in France, apparently for use in medicine. Although they knew of rice and sugar, they did not use them, and oats were regarded as mere horse-fodder.

Within these limitations, the Romans made use of a far wider variety of raw materials than we do today. A banquet might be comparatively simple, as was the one given by the poet Martial: 'My bailiff's wife has brought me mallows, to aid digestion, and other treasures of the garden. Among them are lettuces and leeks for slicing; and there is no lack of mint—the antidote to flatulence —and stimulant elecampane [a cross-bred plant, unknown today]. Slices of egg shall crown anchovies dressed with rue, and there shall be sow's teats swimming in tunny sauce. These will serve as whets for the appetite. My little dinner will all be placed on table at once. There will be a kid snatched from the jaws of the rapacious wolf; there will be titbits such as do not need a carver; there will be beans, and young cabbage sprouts. To these will be added a chicken; and a ham which has already appeared at table three times. For dessert I will give ripe fruits.'

When a host was determined to do things in style, however, he frequently took things to extremes. The satirical genius of Petronius made high comedy out of a feast given by the fictional Trimalchio. The *hors d'œuvre*, which consisted of black and green olives, dormice dipped in honey and rolled in poppyseeds, and miniature sausages, were followed by pepper-seasoned orioles encased in egg-shaped pastry shells. Next came a great tray with 'fat capons and sowbellies and a hare tricked out with wings to look like a little Pegasus. At the corners of the tray stood four little gravy boats, all shaped like the satyr Marsyas, with phalluses for spouts and a spicy hot gravy dripping down over several large fish swimming about in the lagoon of the tray.' The next course was a wild sow of imposing proportions. 'The carver gave a savage slash at the sow's flanks. Under the blow, the flesh parted, the wound burst open and dozens of thrushes came whirring out.' Fortunately, the guests were expected to eat neither the birds nor the sow, but only the dates contained in baskets which hung from the sow's tusks. A vast hog came next, from whose innards spilled link after link of sausages and blood

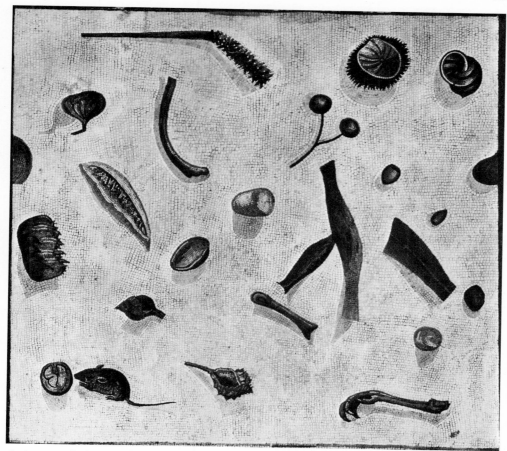

7] A *trompe-l'œil* mosaic floor—'the ill-swept room'—with fish bones, a chicken claw, the shells of crustacea, and fruit kernels

puddings. Then there were fruits and tiny cakes, then a plump chicken and goose eggs for every guest, then pastry thrushes stuffed with nuts and raisins, and quinces pierced all over with thorns so that they looked like sea urchins, and finally what appeared to be a fat goose surrounded by fish and various little birds—all of which were made out of roast pork.

But even Trimalchio's extravagances paled beside the remarkable dish which the emperor Vitellius was later to dedicate to the goddess Minerva. Vitellius, according to Suetonius, was a rather vulgar man who 'thought nothing of snatching lumps of meat or cake off the [sacrificial] altar, almost out of the sacred fire, and bolting them down'. His tribute to Minerva called for pike livers, pheasant brains, peacock brains, flamingo tongues and lamprey roe. Besides being expensive, it must have had rather an unpleasant and paste-like texture—unless these ingredients were offset by others of a less bland consistency. They probably were, since the Romans had a considerable understanding of the refinements of cooking.

Although the very rich had *piscinae*, or fishponds, which kept fresh- or salt-water fish alive until they were needed for table, and aviaries where thrushes were reared to plump perfection on millet, crushed figs and wheat flour, a great deal of the food eaten by most people was certainly less than fresh. The Romans solved the problem by disguising rancidity with spices, fruit, honey, vinegar and wine. Honey and spices were also useful in counteracting the saltiness of fish which had been preserved in brine, and giving flavour to tasteless dried fish or meat. The sweet-sour sauces of modern Italy may well have had their origins in Roman times. One sauce—or base-sauce to which other ingredients were added—was *garum* or *liquamen*. It has not survived, and the recipe may perhaps suggest why. The entrails of one large fish and several smaller ones were, it is said, placed in a container, salted, and then exposed to the sun. When putrescence set in, the liquor was strained off and used as the basis for a relish. This intimidating substance bears a strong family resemblance to *nuoc mam*, the modern Vietnamese fermented fish sauce, which smells appalling but tastes excellent (to the acclimatized palate).

Many Roman recipes—such as that given by Apicius for boiled chicken, which includes vinegar, fig wine, asafoetida, oil, mustard and mint—sound less than appetizing today. Yet modern cookery books frequently recommend dressing fruit with a sauce of mustard, salt, onion, vinegar, sugar, garlic, lemon juice, pepper, oil and tarragon. This unprepossessing combination adds up to nothing more alarming than avocado pear with *vinaigrette* dressing. The key to the matter is quantities. Modern writers specify a pinch of mustard to a pint of oil. Ancient writers did not, and as a result the reader tends to assume *equal* quantities of all the ingredients specified—which would make nonsense of even the most delicious dish. Some Roman foods, particularly the sausages, cheeses and small songbirds they were so fond of, must have been excellent.

The Romans were as inventive with their bread as with their composite dishes. A rich man giving a banquet to a poet would have the bread baked in lyre shape. At a wedding, it might take the form of linked rings. 'In some places', said Pliny, 'bread is called after the dishes eaten with it, such as oyster-bread, in others from its special delicacy, as cake-bread, in others from the short time spent in making it, as hasty-bread, and also from the method of

8] A bakery in Roman times

baking, as oven bread, or tin loaf, or baking pan bread. . . . Some use eggs
or milk in kneading the dough, while even butter has been used by races
enjoying peace, when attention can be devoted to variety in pastry-making.'
There were many types of cake, too, and the Romans were infinitely fond of
cheesecake—though it would be misleading to assume that cheese was always
numbered among the ingredients. It seems more likely that the name derived

from the consistency of the cake, which may have been a moist, spongy mixture with a texture like cream cheese. Chrysippus of Tyana, in his *Art of making bread*, gave a recipe for a kind of cheesecake made in Crete. 'Take some Thasian and Pontic nuts and some almonds, and also a poppy. Roast this last with great care, and then take the seed and pound it in a clean mortar; then, adding the fruits which I have mentioned above, beat them up with boiled honey, putting in plenty of pepper, and make the whole into a soft mass (but it will be of a black colour because of the poppy); flatten it and make it into a square shape; then, having pounded some white sesame, soften that too with boiled honey, and draw it out into two cakes, placing one beneath [the poppy-seed mixture] and the other above, so as to have the black surface in the middle, and make it into a neat shape.'

Professional bakers came late to Rome. According to Pliny, 'there were no bakers at Rome down to the war with king Perseus [171–168 BC]. . . . The citizens used to make bread themselves, and this was especially the task of the women, as it is even now in most nations . . . Nor used people to have cooks on their regular staff of servants, but they hired them from the provision market.' Once a beginning had been made, however, members of the bakers' guilds became very important people.

Wine, like bread, was a staple item in the Roman diet. There were at least eighty good native wines, as well as wines produced from imported vinestock. There were dark red, clear red, golden and white wines which, when aged, became syrupy and concentrated. Young wines were improved by the judicious addition of mature wine, and it was rare for the Romans to drink their wine undiluted—they nearly always added a good proportion of water. Sometimes the vintners added liquid resin and vine ash to the grape juice before fermenting, or a mixture of herbs, spices and sea-water which had been aged for some years. The wine was kept to mature in pitch-coated jars in a loft above the *fumarium*, the room where wood was seasoned, and cheese, ham and other delicacies left to smoke.

Suetonius claimed that the decline of the Roman empire was a result of apathy and gluttony, and recent research suggests that this may have been true in a rather different sense. Roman wine merchants preserved and sweetened wine by adding to it a syrup made from unfermented grape juice boiled down in lead-lined pots. Well-to-do Roman kitchens used lead cooking pots and cups in place of the earthenware utensils of the poor. Water-pipes, cosmetics and paint all included lead. Over a period, the Roman upper classes must have absorbed lead in appreciable quantities. And the results of lead poisoning, if chronic, are anaemia and loss of weight (which may be equated with Suetonius' apathy), constipation (of which the Romans constantly complained), and loss of appetite (which may explain, at least in part, their preoccupation with tempting and unusual dishes). Lead poisoning also induces miscarriages, stillbirths and sterility. Literary and census information shows that the number of aristocratic births was very low indeed—and that most of the rich died young.

As the numbers of rich diminished, the numbers of poor increased. Small farmers drifted discontentedly to the towns. Even in the days of Julius Caesar, it was necessary to dispense free grain to 200,000 unemployed. By the time of Aurelian (AD 270–75), the number had risen to 300,000, each of whom received two breads, or small loaves, daily. The name given to the urban unemployed was *plebs frumentaria*, i.e. corn commoners. Since most landowners had given up corn production in favour of more profitable cattle and sheep, Rome had to drain wheat from Egypt, North Africa and even distant Britain. The emperor Tiberius did his best for a time to enforce economy. 'The aediles [magistrates]', said Suetonius, 'were to restrict the amount of food offered for sale in cookshops and eating-houses; even banning breadstuffs. And to set an example in his campaign against waste he often served, at formal dinner parties, half-eaten dishes left over from the day before—or only one side of a wild boar, sliced down the backbone—which he said contained everything that the other side did.'

Even such poor fare as that would have been welcome to the family of five described by the poet Alexis:

> Yet, alas! alas! have we
> Nourishment for only three!
> Two must therefore often make
> Scanty meal on barley cake . . .
> And our best and daintiest cheer,
> Throughout the bright half of the year,
> Is but acorns, beans, chick-peas,
> Cabbage, lupins, radishes,
> Onions, wild pears nine or ten,
> And a grasshopper now and then.

Three

By the second century A D, the Roman empire was on the defensive. By the fourth century, Constantinople, not Rome, was the imperial capital.

Persians, Arabs and Berbers on the eastern and southern borders disturbed the peace in varying degree. But it was to the north that the great threat lay—the nomadic hordes of the Goths, the Vandals and, for a period in the middle of the fifth century, the Huns, whose empire stretched from the Caspian in the east to the Low Countries in the west. Their numbers were not, perhaps, as great as the word 'horde' would suggest, but they were infinitely mobile and each band gave the impression of being in several places at once. Roman legionaries travelled on foot. The nomads (men, women and children) were mounted. Their homes and their few belongings were transported in supply wagons, and they drove their cattle—their food—along with them. The cattle supplied meat, milk and cheese. When the nomads wanted grain, they raided settled communities for it, or simply pitched their tents in one place for a year, sowed oats, gathered the harvest, and then moved on.

When the Visigoths and the Huns swept into western Europe, France was already impoverished and disrupted. But the virile and frequently destructive newcomers brought a breath of air into the stifling atmosphere of Roman Gaul. Under the Romans, the French economy had been rigidly commercialized, with a caste system as unyielding as that of India. A baker, for example, could not change his trade under any circumstances, and his heirs —whether heirs of the body or not—had to follow in his footsteps. The economy of the Goths and Huns, however, and of their successors, the Burgundians and Franks, had scarcely progressed beyond the barter stage. The centuries that followed were to be centuries of adjustment on both sides.

Italy, too, was prey to barbarian invasions, but it was during the period known as the Dark Ages that Venice laid the foundations of her commercial supremacy in European trade. Salt was the great profit-earner in the early stages. In the year 500, Cassiodorus, minister to the Ostrogothic king of Italy, wrote in flattering but perceptive terms to the Maritime Tribunes of Venice. In 'the famous Venetia', he said, 'fish alone is abundant; rich and poor live there on equal terms. A single food nourishes all alike. . . . All your rivalry is expended in your salt works; in place of ploughs and sickles you turn your drying pans, and hence comes all your gain, and what you have made is your very own.... It may well be that there are some men who seek not gold, but there lives no man who does not need salt, which seasons all our food.'

A natural development of the salt trade was a trade in salted fish. And after salted fish came salted meat. However dark conditions were in Europe, trade never really stopped by land or sea. Armed caravans set out from France or Italy, joining up with others on the way. At certain periods, these commercial caravans became so powerful that they almost took on the appearance of military expeditions. Certainly, they interfered in the affairs of, for example, the valley of the Danube, Bohemia and Carinthia, at the same time as they sold German carpentry-work, Black Sea grain and Byzantine art objects to the inhabitants. Nothing stopped the merchants. Hungarians, Bulgarians, Poles, Germans, Spaniards, the Flemish and the English, all flocked to Venice and Amalfi to buy and sell. When, as in the bitter winter of 860, the lagoons froze, the merchants covered the last stages by wagon instead of boat. Venice, a natural centre for trade between east and west, exported salt and salted meat to Constantinople and brought back in return cloves, cinnamon, pepper, saffron, ginger, cardamom, sugar and dye-stuffs which had come from Asia by the spice routes established centuries before.

Scarcely had Europe come to terms with the nomadic hordes than a new and much more intransigent force came into being. Under the inspiration of Muhammad, the Arabs began to sweep through the lands of the unbelievers. Little over a century after the death of the Prophet in 632, the Umayyad

9] A monastery of *c.* 1000. The strapwork decoration is barbarian in influence, but the vivarium in the foreground (for keeping fish alive until they were needed) represents settled civilization, careful man with a store-cupboard

Caliphate ruled what had been the Persian empire, Egypt, the coast of North Africa, almost the whole of Spain and much of the Languedoc. A hundred years later, they had a foothold on Sicily, too. Though, by a strange series of historical accidents, the Arabs were to be able to give back to Europe the Greek learning which had been lost in the collapse of the classical world, and though they contributed much of their own in art and architecture, medicine and mathematics, they introduced little new to the diet of their conquered territories. If anything, they reduced the variety of foodstuffs although improving cultivation methods. Their own basic diet was barley, mutton (roasted, or in spiced barley stews), dates and sheep's milk. The Prophet had forbidden intoxicating liquors and pork, and in the lands of Islam vinestocks were destroyed and the pig became a rarity.

While much of the western world seemed to bristle with swords and spears, Christian monasteries were beginning to establish themselves as oases of calm. There, what remained of Roman civilization was cross-fertilized by the religious and social precepts of Christianity. The art of the monasteries was part Byzantine, part barbarian; their organization was Christian; their food and agriculture simplified Roman; and their position in the social order new and influential. In the late eighth and early ninth centuries, history is briefly illuminated by the reign of Charlemagne, and French monastic life of the period is comparatively well documented.

Monasteries and the estates of great noblemen were run on similar lines—as part farm, part business house, and part trade school. The monasteries were perhaps the more efficient. From everyone who worked or lived on the land, certain taxes were exacted. Every man who worked his own rented piece of land had also to provide his labour when it was demanded by his monastic or lay masters. He might also have to pay with livestock or grain for the right to pasture his animals on his masters' land. There was, furthermore, a kind of personal tax.

Large estates were divided into manageable units, each run by a steward, and Charlemagne's instructions to his own senior stewards give a very fair indication of the productive capacity of such units as well as of the type of food consumed by the rich during this period. Each Christmas, the stewards were required to provide their emperor with 'clear and methodical' accounts so that he might know the extent of his possessions—'the number of pigs, of quit-rents, of obligations and reparations; that of game taken in the woods without our permission . . . that of markets, of vines, and of those who owe us wine; the reckoning of hay . . . that of vegetables, of millet, of wool, of flax, of hemp; that of tree-fruits, of walnut trees and other nut trees, of grafted trees of all kinds; that of turnips; that of fish-ponds . . . that of honey, of wax, of fat, of tallow and of soap; of mulberry wine, of cooked [thickened] wine, of hydromel [spiced and sweetened honey wine], of vinegar, of beer, of new wine and old wine; that of new corn and old corn; that of chickens and eggs; that of geese.' Sheep, goats, cheese, butter, smoked meats and salt meats are also mentioned. In the case of oxen, it was only the lame which were to be killed for food, lest the plough should stand idle.

According to Abbot Eginhard, a churchman who was secretary to the emperor, Charlemagne himself was temperate in eating and drinking. 'His daily meal was served in four courses only, exclusive of the roast, which the hunters used to bring in on spits, and which he ate with more pleasure than any other food.' The extent of the imperial household was considerable. A monk of the monastery of St Gall, who wrote a life of the emperor in the ninth century, recorded that 'while Charles was eating, he was waited upon by dukes and rulers and kings of various [tributary] peoples; and when his banquet was ended then those who served him fed, and they were served by counts and praefects and nobles of different ranks. And when these last had made an end of eating, then came the military officers and scholars of the palace, then the chiefs of the various departments of the palace, then their subordinates, then the servants of those servants. So that the last comers did not get a mouthful of food before the middle of the night.'

Charlemagne's stewards, like the monks of the new foundations, probably relied heavily on a fourth-century manual of agriculture—Palladius *On Husbandry*—for their farming methods and techniques. Indeed, Palladius was still being used as a textbook in England in the fifteenth century, and not a very suitable one since it applied more to Mediterranean than northern conditions. It would be interesting to know just how closely Charlemagne's

The simplest of ploughs, cultivation of the vine, and three sinners—one in the stocks, the other two chained to pillars

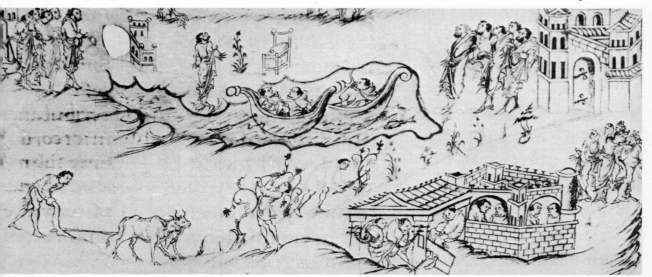

11] The Normans boiled their food in a cauldron or cooked it on a spit, methods which had been used in Europe for hundreds of years and were to be used for hundreds of years more

hydromel resembled that of Palladius. 'For mead, at the rising of the dog-star add a pint of skimmed honey to six of clear water. In boilers let naked children shake it five hours to and fro, vessel and all. Afterwards in the sun, with forty days' standing it is done.' In Charlemagne's day, spices were probably added (which would change the flavour), and the children were probably clothed (which would not). Palladius was very informative on viticulture and allied techniques. He gave instructions on how to make wine clear, and how to make new wine appear old. To make a mild wine strong, he suggested: 'Take peppercorns ten, and twice as many pistachio nuts. With a quantity of wine, stamp them as small as you may, and add the mixture to six pints of wine and shake it so that all comes together. Then let it rest and filter it and no man will refuse it.'

In time, the monasteries—with their vines, their ponds of live fish to provide sustenance on meatless days, their extensive herb and physic gardens —became centres of local industry and commerce. They had their own commercial travellers, who sold their produce at favourable terms in distant markets and bought iron or amber or spices in exchange. The monks exacted tribute from the towns that tended to cluster for safety around their gates. The market town of St Riquier, for example, supplied the abbey of Centule. Its bakers were expected to provide the abbey with a hundred breads a week, the butchers with thirty gallons of fat or tallow a week, the wine merchants

with thirty-two gallons of wine and one of oil a week, and the tavern-keepers with sixty gallons of ale a day. Other trades provided for the other needs of the monastery—clothes, skins, wooden goods, cooking-pots, materials for the manuscripts which are almost all that remain today of the world of the Dark Ages.

After Charlemagne, the Frankish empire shrank, and the light of revived culture seemed to fade. Hunger was endemic, and famine a commonplace. In the year 943, around Limoges, it is said that forty thousand people died of St Anthony's Fire, or ergotism. Ergot is a disease of rye, and makes the grain black and sweet. In the tenth century, people would not normally have used any food which seemed strange in appearance—but in a time of hunger everyday inhibitions disappear. The tainted rye was made into flour and bread, and people began to die in the streets—screaming, mad—their skin inflamed beyond bearing (hence the name St Anthony's 'fire'). A smell of decay hung over the countryside. And because this was the tenth century, everyone thought the smell was the cause of the pestilence.

In France and Germany during the ninth and tenth centuries, cannibalism was rife. There was nothing personal about it. A man did not knowingly eat his neighbour. But demand always produces supply. Killer bands roamed the countryside, attacked travellers, cooked their flesh and sold it in the nearest market. They may have called it mutton—even 'two-legged mutton', as the

Chinese did in the twelfth century when there was famine in the northern provinces. There, however, some sections of society consciously acquired a taste for it, and it is recorded that dishes made from the flesh of old men, women, girls and children each had a special name, and presumably a special flavour. Cannibalism persisted in Bohemia, Silesia and Poland until the end of the Middle Ages, and was probably the truth behind the werewolf legends.

While hungry Swedes ate biscuit made from a little flour and a lot of reindeer blood; while hungry Frenchmen lived on acorn-bread; while an English lord and lady were still known by their uncorrupted titles of *hlaford* (loaf-keeper) and *hlaefdigge* (kneader of dough); while land trade routes were still dangerous and largely unprofitable—the sea routes flourished. Between them, in the south, Venetians and Arabs had the spice trade in their grasp. In the north, the Frisians first and then the Vikings and Varangians stretched their tentacles from the Caspian to Iceland, trading in fish, wine and beer, salt from the Crimea and honey from the principalities of Russia.

In the duchy of Normandy, Viking blood mingled with the blood of the Franks, and the eleventh century saw a great outburst of Norman enterprise. Even before the Conquest, a Norman adventurer had seized the district of Salerno in Italy—and with it one of the most famous medical schools in history, where Greek, Roman and Arab medicine all met. When the Crusades began, noble Crusaders on the way to free the holy places from the rule of the pagans found Salerno a convenient and comfortable place in which to recruit their strength for the perils to come. Frequently they returned by the same route, particularly if they had sustained some wound or infection. With such elevated patronage, the influence of Salerno spread wide. Its teachings are of particular interest in their relation to diet, for the so-called 'humoral doctrine' of Salerno—derived almost directly from the theories of Galen and Hippocrates nine hundred years before—formed the basis of European medicine for another five hundred years to come.

In the days when knowledge was simple enough to be explained simply, it was the custom to cast it in the form of verse, so that the uninitiated might remember it more easily. This was the case with the *Salerno Regimen of Health* (Regimen Sanitatis Salernitanum). The humoral doctrine was explained as follows:

> Four humours reign within our bodies wholly,
> And these comparèd to four elements,
> The *Sanguine*, *Choler*, *Phlegm*, and *Melancholy* . . .

Like air both warm and moist, is *Sanguine* clear,
Like fire doth *Choler* hot and dry appear.
Like water cold and moist is *Phlegmatic*,
The *Melancholy* cold, dry earth is like.

Now though we give these humours several names,
Yet all men are of all participant,
But all have not in quantity the same,
For some in some are more predominant.

The crucial point was that foods also possessed these various humours, and judicious adjustment of diet and temperament could work wonders. Cheese was accounted a heavy, cold food, very suitable for hot, dry 'choleric' temperaments, but to be avoided by people of cold, moist 'phlegmatic' type.

12] An angel offers a lemon to the Holy Child. According to dietetic theory, this was most ill-advised, but in Renaissance art the lemon represented, not citrus fruit, but fidelity in love

All children were assumed to be phlegmatic. Fruit, therefore, which was cold and moist, was fundamentally bad for them—but it is worth noting that, in art, symbolism triumphed over dietetic theory and artists frequently showed angels offering fruit to the Holy Child.

The idea that there was an association between food and temperament was not new even in Galen's time. The Indian *Bhagavadgita* (second century B C) had, in fact, remarked on it, though from a somewhat different standpoint. 'The foods that are dear to men of the goodness-mood are moist, oily, firm, and cordial. . . . The foods dear to men of the mood of fieriness are bitter, sour, salty.'

Many other attitudes to food recur throughout history, in all countries and all centuries. In particular, references to garlic still strike a chord today. The Indian Brahmins, the priestly caste, were forbidden to eat it. The Prophet Muhammad, when he refused a dish containing garlic, explained disarmingly: 'I am a man who has close contact with others.' The school of Salerno had something to say on the matter, too—but on the other side:

> Six things, that here in order shall ensue,
> Against all poisons have a secret power,
> *Pear, Garlic, Radish-roots, Nuts, Rape* and *Rue.*
> But *Garlic* chief. For they that it devour,
> May drink, and care not who their drink do brew;
> May walk in airs infected every hour.
> Since *Garlic* then hath powers to save from death,
> Bear with it though it make unsavoury breath,
> And scorn not *Garlic*, like to some that think
> It only makes men wink, and drink, and stink!

Four

In the thirteenth century, the Sieur de Joinville accompanied Louis IX of France on campaigns in Egypt and the Holy Land. He was greatly impressed by the productiveness of the river Nile. 'Before the river enters into Egypt, people who are accustomed to do so cast their nets outspread into the river at night; and when morning comes, they find in their nets . . . ginger, rhubarb, wood of aloes, and cinnamon. And it is said that these things come from the earthly paradise.'

More probably they were flotsam from the loading points at which eastern cargoes were transferred from camel caravans to Nile barges for shipment to Alexandria. But in the thirteenth century, and for some time afterwards, few people had any clear idea of where the ginger, the rhubarb, the wood of aloes, and the cinnamon which played so large a part in mediaeval trade came

13] A sixteenth-century view of the perils of the spice trade. A very small camel caravan is attacked by armed horsemen

from. Spices and pharmaceutical ingredients—amongst which rhubarb and aloes-wood were included—had been brought from the east since at least as early as the fourteenth century BC. By the time they had made their lengthy journey, however, passing through many different hands, all notion of their origins was lost. It was known that they came from the east, but 'the east' began at the end of the Mediterranean and stretched away to the end of the world. In some cases, the European name for a particular product might echo its name in the language of the country from which it was imported. Pepper, for example, from the Sanskrit *pippali*; ginger from *sringavera*; rice probably from the Tamil *arisi*. But who, in Europe in the Middle Ages, knew—or even knew of—these Indian languages? As long as the Arab middlemen were cooperative and not intolerably grasping, no one greatly cared where the vital spices came from. The important thing was that they came at all.

Why were these spices so important? It is generally accepted that they were used by the rich of Europe—for the poor could not afford them—to disguise the flavour of tainted meat and to lend flavour to tasteless meat. Within limitations, this is true, but it is by no means as universal as some authorities suggest. The everyday diet of the rich who lived on their estates (as most of them did) consisted of small game birds and small animals. Unless the household was very large, there was no question of killing an ox or a pig and then

14] In the Middle Ages, only the strongest young animals could survive the poor fodder of winter. The rest which they and their families enjoyed the last fresh meat they would eat for several months. The other events s

eating beef or pork every day until it was finished. When large animals were slaughtered, part was eaten fresh and the rest was preserved by either salting or drying. There is no reason to believe that fresh meat was any less tasty than it is today, although it may have been tougher. Dried meat, however, certainly needed the aid of spices to make it palatable, and most people lived on dried meat in the winter, since it was the custom to slaughter all except the sturdiest farm animals in late autumn because of the lack of good winter fodder. Fish was a different matter; in summer, the fish that was eaten on meatless days in such parts of the country as had no productive rivers and streams may indeed have been a trifle high and in need of the disguise of spices.

It was as towns grew up, however, that the need for spices really made itself felt. The rich often had to spend part of the year in town—whether it was imperial Rome or London in the Middle Ages. Much of their food would be supplied by their country estates, and would be none too fresh by the time it arrived at a rate of four miles per hour (maximum) over bad roads. As the towns grew, too, the number of well-to-do burghers and merchants increased. Many of them lived in town the whole year round, and had to buy their food (often illegally) from farmers outside the city limits, or (legally) from trades-men within them. As time passed, the cities had to draw on suppliers farther and farther away, and 'fresh' food became progressively less fresh by the time it reached the customer. Nevertheless, until a very late date, the population of Europe was a rural population and it is fair to assume that, though Euro-peans customarily used spices to liven up dried meats and fish, and to a lesser extent (mainly in towns) to disguise rancidity, they also used them for the

ntered in November or December, and their owners took advantage of the occasion to hold great feasts at s tapestry are in July: haymaking; August: reaping; September: ploughing and sowing; and October: the vintage

very simple reason that they liked the taste. There is no other way of accounting for the enormous quantities that were consumed.

In Europe, the poor had to make do with herbs from the garden and the hedgerow if they wanted to vary the monotony of their diet. In India and China, however, they were more fortunate. From very early times, their diet —as in European countries—had been based on grain. In the Indus valley civilization (c. 2500–1500 BC), the grain was wheat or barley, but on the other side of India, in the Ganges valley, rice was grown. Little is known about the Ganges peoples, but the Indus cities of Mohenjodaro and Harappa have been excavated. There, spice-grinding stones were found.

Unleavened wheat or barley cakes make a monotonous staple diet. So, too, does boiled rice. It appears that, even in these early days, the Indians concocted savoury relishes of meat, fish, fruit or vegetables mixed with crushed spices to improve their basic fare. Meat and fish were difficult to come by, and a mouthful of meat cooked plainly would have contributed very little to a diet of barley cake or boiled rice. But a dash of spicy sauce (curry) with each mouthful transformed the whole meal. Better still, the sauce was capable of infinite variation from day to day. The Indus valley peoples also domesticated the buffalo, the goat and the sheep, which provided them with milk, curds and ghee (clarified butter)—then, as always, an essential part of the Indian diet. It seems probable that the Indian peasant of those days was, both dietetically and gastronomically, better off than his contemporaries of Sumer and Egypt, who subsisted on bread, onions and beer.

The Indus valley civilizations were destroyed over a period of time by barbarian invaders—the light-skinned nomadic Aryans, who felt superior to the dark and peaceable people they had conquered. It was many centuries before the conquerors learned to value the foods and customs of the land they had settled in. By 800 BC, however, they had rediscovered wheat and sugarcane, and described barley and rice as 'the two immortal sons of heaven'. They ate barley porridge, barley gruel, and barley cakes with ghee; they grew five varieties of rice, and ate them with curds, ghee, sesame, beans or meat. Sometimes they roasted the meat on spits, sometimes they boiled it with rice—into that half porridge, half stew which features in the cuisine of all nations at some stage (the English version was made with hulled wheat and known as frumenty, or furmity)—sometimes they fried it in a mixture of ghee and soma juice, the sap of a mountain plant. Like other nations, India had its beer, too, made from fermented barley. This was known as *sura*.

By 500 BC, south India was exporting rice, pepper and peacocks to Babylon, Egypt and Greece. At home, turmeric and pepper were used for the curries that accompanied rice and barley cakes, as well as sea salt, black salt, rock salt, red salt, earth salt, cumin, ginger, cloves, vinegar and (as in Rome) asafoetida —known in India as *hing*, and sometimes used in the barley cakes themselves instead of in the curry. Since India was fortunate in having sugarcane as well as honey, a taste had begun to grow for sweet dishes. *Sikharini* was a popular one, made of curds, crystal sugar and spices. Alexander the Great was astonished to see reeds from which the Indians extracted all the honey they wanted, but when sugar finally came to Europe it was treated more as a medicine than as a honey-substitute.

The Aryan invaders, once they had settled in the country, began to stabilize a class structure—with themselves at the top. They were determined to maintain their separate identity, and one of the methods they used offers a curious variant on the sumptuary legislation which crops up over and over again in history and is usually designed to curb extravagance or to keep inferiors in their place. Many sumptuary laws forbid the poor to eat what the rich eat. In India, it was the Aryan rulers who were forbidden to eat certain of the foods favoured by their non-Aryan subjects. Beans, garlic, onions, mush-

rooms and turnips were forbidden for many years, and the prohibition on garlic
and onions has never really been abandoned. According to the Chinese traveller, Hsüan-Ch'uang, those who wished to eat such strong-smelling foods had
to do so *outside* the town. Many orthodox Hindus today still refuse to eat garlic.

In the eighth century B C, it was still permissible for non-Aryans to cook
for their Aryan masters as long as they shaved, trimmed their nails, and
bathed beforehand. As time passed, however, taboos increased. Food which
had been handled by 'unworthy persons' was regarded as unclean. The
'unworthy', in the early stages, included moneylenders, eunuchs, tavern-
keepers and spies; misers and prisoners were later added to this list; and so,
ultimately, were prostitutes, atheists, and henpecked husbands. 'Unclean'
meat was prohibited—i.e. meat which had been cut with a sword, dog meat,
human meat, the meat of the scavenging village pig, that of carnivorous
animals, locusts, camels, and of hairless or excessively hairy animals. Brahmins
(the priestly caste) and students were forbidden intoxicating liquor, while
Kshatriyas (the warrior caste) and Vaisyas (the merchant caste) were permitted
the grape but not the grain. In other words, they could drink honey-, flower-,
fruit- or molasses-based liquors but not those made from cereals.

In the sixth century B C, two new religions appeared in India, propagated
by the Buddha and by Mahavira. Vegetarianism is a recurring theme in India,
and the teachings of the Buddha and Mahavira encouraged it. But while the
Buddha contented himself with advising his followers not to permit meat to
be killed specially for them, Mahavira forbade his followers (the Jains) to eat
even fruit or vegetables without first making sure that they contained no
living thing. The ban on killing was not the result of any sentimental belief in
kindness to animals, but part of the doctrine of transmigration of souls. When
a living thing dies, if it has lived its life well its soul is reincarnated at a higher
level; if badly, at a lower one. Even an insect, therefore, contains what may
have been and may again become a human soul. A very similar doctrine was
being preached at much the same time by the followers of Pythagoras in
classical Greece. They took the matter even further; there was a long-standing
connection in the ancient mind between beans and ghosts, and the Pytha-
goreans abstained from beans as well as from more obviously animate objects.

Buddhism and Jainism gave religious sanction to a vegetarian diet, and it
seems possible that, in times of dearth, Indian rulers made use of this sanction
to give a voluntary and honourable complexion to what were, in fact, simple
food shortages. Near centres of Buddhism and Jainism, vegetarianism was a
very real principle, but elsewhere it waxed and waned according to the

15] A garden in Kashmir. Among other produce can be seen apples, melons and grapes; kohlrabi, radishes, asparagus and aubergines

political and social climate. When the emperor Asoka was converted to Buddhism, for example, he decreed that not more than two peacocks and one gazelle should be killed for the royal table, and not every day. By the end of his reign, he had forbidden the slaughter of any living thing. This may indicate that his beliefs grew stronger as he grew older. It may, on the other hand, indicate that many food animals were in danger of becoming extinct and that only a rigid policy of preservation would allow them to survive and multiply. The idea of a close season on game was not new, and it still applies in Britain today—notably to game birds, deer and salmon. The ban on cow slaughter, however, has different roots. In India, as in the Egypt of the Pharaohs and the Europe of Charlemagne, the cow and the ox were valuable animals. In the days before the steam engine, muscle was the only source of power, and cattle were the draught-animals *par excellence*. But they were slow to reproduce themselves and not always easy to feed in arid lands. It was hardly surprising that the people of almost all early civilizations should have guarded them well. In India this was particularly the case, since the Indian diet leans heavily on the milk, curds and butter which the cow provides.

While some of the Indian poor were feasting on cold barley cakes, fried beans, shrivelled grain, barley stew, barley water, sour gruel and the scum from boiled rice, the administrative handbook known as the *Arthasastra—*

16] This detail from a badly damaged fresco in the caves of
Ajanta shows a merchant selling food, probably curds, in
the bazaar. Seventh century

which dates from the first centuries of the Christian era and is usually attributed to the earlier statesman, Kautilya—listed approved quantities of food
for different persons.

> 'One prastha [21 oz] of rice grains, a quarter [as much] broth, an amount of
> salt [equal to] one sixteenth of the broth, butter and oil [equal to] a quarter
> of the broth; these constitute one meal of an Arya[n] male.
> One sixth [of a prastha] of broth, and half the quantity of fat is [enough]
> for the lower classes.'

Women were assumed to need only three-quarters of the given quantities,
and children half. If, in fact, many people actually did consume such large
quantities of rice at one sitting, rice production must have had some difficulty

in keeping up with the demand. But there is a problem. It is not easy to judge what ancient Roman food tasted like because Roman recipes did not specify quantities. The recipes in the *Arthasastra* do specify quantities—but in words whose precise meaning we do not know. One ancient Indian text, the *Code of Manu*, has led historians to equate the *prastha* with a 21-oz measure, the *pala* with a 1⅓-oz measure, and so on. By this reading, an *Arthasastra* recipe for a curry to accompany rice is, to say the least, odd—27 oz of meat and 27 oz of spices are to be mixed with insignificant quantities of fat, salt and sugar, and a mere 10½ oz of curds. It must be assumed that, just as foodstuffs varied widely in different parts of India, so too did weights and measures.

In the early centuries of the present era, Indians apparently ate two meals a day. Householders were advised that, if their work was to be performed efficiently, each of these main meals should consist of thirty-two mouthfuls. It was further suggested that the stomach should be considered as divided into four separate parts; the aim should be to fill two parts with food and one part with liquid; the remaining part was to be left empty—for the movement of wind.

The Indian meal was surrounded by ritual and caste usage. No matter how many servants there were in the household, it was the wife's task to prepare her husband's food and serve it to him. He, before seating himself, would remove his head-dress and sandals and have the dirt and dust of the streets washed from his feet by his children or by a servant. His chair was a wicker stool only seven inches high, and he sat on it with his legs crossed before him, while his wife placed a tray in front of him containing one or two pieces of ginger and some salt as an appetizer. After this, there might be boiled rice and bean soup and hot butter sauce, then cakes with ghee, fruit, and sugarcane to chew.

The rich had tables rather than trays. In the tenth century, an Arab merchant who had visited India said: 'As for Indian princes and great men, it is the custom in India to place before them each day tables made with interlaced leaves of the cocoa palm; with these same leaves, they make kinds of plates and dishes. At mealtime, the food is served on these interlaced leaves and, when the meal is finished, the table and leaf plates are thrown into the water with whatever may remain of the food. They disdain to have the same things served up the next day.' Ritual demanded that food should have no contact with impurity (and it may be mentioned here that, in hot climates, ritual and hygiene very often go hand in hand). Porous, unglazed earthenware, the usual pottery material of the time, could never be wholly cleaned after it had once been used, unless it were re-fired, so most Indians used thick, unabsorbent leaves as platters and threw them away afterwards.

In India, rich men in the early Middle Ages sat down to almost as many courses as their contemporaries in Europe. Indian food, however, was rather more varied, since Europeans were still wary of fruit and had not learned to make the most of dairy products. At a banquet given by King Srenika, one of India's mediaeval rulers, the menu began with pomegranates, grapes and jujubes (not the rubbery confections of twentieth-century Europe, but a fruit resembling the date). These were followed by oranges, which are native to India and China, mangoes, dates and pieces of sugarcane. Then came cooked dishes, perhaps including *kosali*, delicate mouthfuls of spiced roast meat rolled first in meat pounded to a paste and then in rice, and cooked over the fire. After the cooked dishes there were sweet cakes, then spicy boiled rice, then broth. At this stage, the plates were removed and the royal hands washed. Next came perfumed dishes of curds, after which the royal hands were washed once more. The final course was a rich liquor made from milk, somewhat reduced by boiling, then sweetened with sugar and honey, and tinted with saffron.

Handwashing was not only a ritual but a necessity. Indians, like Europeans at the same period, ate with their fingers, although Europeans sometimes supplemented their fingers with the pointed knives they used for everything from pruning bushes to paring fingernails. The Indian's general-purpose blade was the machete, large, square at the tip, and ill adapted as an aid to dining. Instead, Indians often used *chapatis* as a scoop to transfer rice and curry to their mouths. The *chapati* is a thin unleavened pancake made of wheat flour kneaded with water and salt and cooked on a hot surface. It is another of those foods which emphasize the similarity of cooking techniques in widely divergent civilizations. The Mexican *tortilla* and the Scots oatcake are both made on much the same principle and in much the same way. But because the *chapati* is made from wheat, the *tortilla* from maize, and the oatcake from oats (in each case the commonest food grain of the area concerned), the final results are very different. The great advantage of the *chapati* as a dining scoop was, of course, that both scoop and rice could be eaten together if *chapatis* were plentiful; if not, one *chapati* would have to last throughout the meal, but it could still be eaten at the end, by which time it was impregnated with all the delicious flavours that had gone before.

While the rest of the world ate mainly with its fingers, the Chinese had achieved the happy solution of chopsticks, product of the bamboo tree which

17] In India, a royal servant rolls out *chapatis*

provided China with an infinite variety of useful objects. Chopsticks are excellently adapted to many purposes, taking the place of knife, fork, spoon and tongs. With chopsticks a Chinese diner can scoop rice to his mouth, or pick up a single appetizing morsel from among many, or tear the tender flesh from a roast bird, or hold a small joint firmly while he bites it. Chinese-style cooking and chopsticks suit each other, and which came first is one of the great unanswerable questions. Certainly chopsticks would make little impression on a baron of beef or a plate of bacon and eggs.

In the second millennium BC, Chinese agriculture was as well organized as in Sumer or Egypt. Many crops were grown extensively. One of the odes in the eighth-century BC *She King* describes the year's produce in 1700 BC:

> In the sixth month they eat sparrow plums and grapes;
> In the seventh, they cook the *k'wei* [vegetables] and pulse;
> In the eighth, they knock down the dates;
> In the tenth, they reap the rice
> And make the spirits [rice-liquor] for the spring . . .[1]
> In the seventh month, they eat the melons;
> In the eighth, they cut down the bottle-gourds;
> In the ninth, they gather the hempseed.

[1] For consumption only by the aged.

When the rice had been harvested, it was bruised in mortars to free the husks, then winnowed or sieved. The husks were probably collected and sold to goldsmiths, who used them for polishing gems. The Chinese, unlike other nations, do not, in the early days, seem to have favoured boiling as a cooking method. As early as the eighth century BC, they had evolved the technique of steaming rice. Nor is there much early mention of spices and flavourings other than pepper, ginger, salt and liquorice. But with roast turtle and minced carp, grilled sturgeon and bream, wild duck or hare stew, spit-roasted pheasant, chicken or crane (to mention only a few of the delicacies referred to in the *She King*), perhaps they had no need of spices. The fact that so many different fruits were indigenous to China, or were cultivated there from a very early date—including the peach, pear, plum, cherry, jujube, chestnut, melon, mulberry, medlar and tangerine—might possibly account for the occasional sweet-sour sauces which figure in the Chinese cuisine. Dairy farming has never been a feature of Chinese life, and even today milk, cream and butter are very rarely used. Thus milk, one of the ever-recurring ingredients in Western sauces, was denied the Chinese cook. If boiled food was rare, so was

18] Food is chopped and prepared in a kitchen hung with fish and poultry, and servants rush past carrying trays and cups to their master and his guests. Banquet in a Chinese nobleman's house *c.* 200 BC to AD 200

stock. And rice wine and soy sauce do not lend themselves to being used as the sole liquid in any but comparatively dry dishes—although soy sauce may have been much milder in early times. It is possible, therefore, that fruit juices may have been used as an alternative to water in some cases, with vinegar or soy added to temper their sweetness.

Although alcohol had been banned to all but the aged in 1700 BC, by the year 800 BC or thereabouts drunkenness was as much of a problem in China as it was in Egypt. As the *She King* reprovingly said:

> When the guests have drunk too much,
> They shout out and brawl.
> They disorder the dishes;
> They keep dancing in a fantastic manner.
> Thus when they have drunk too much
> They become insensible of their errors.
> With their caps on one side and like to fall off
> They keep dancing, and will not stop. . . .
>
> Drinking is a good institution
> Only when there is good deportment in it.

Two thousand years later, Marco Polo said that the spiced rice wine of Cathay was 'better to drink than any other wine'.

By Marco Polo's time, many dynasties had come and gone. The population had increased to sixty millions, and large parts of the country were ruled by the Mongols (the Yüan dynasty). The imperial capital had earlier been at Kaifeng in northern China, but had moved south to Hangchow at the time of the first barbarian invasions, taking with it cooks accustomed to the vinegary northern cuisine. In Hangchow, vinegary northern cooking met salty southern cooking and the new capital, with its very large population, began to cater for all tastes. There were restaurants, hotels, taverns and tea houses, each with its own speciality. Mother Sung's fish soup was famous. 'Every day', said Marco Polo, 'a vast quantity of fish is brought upstream from the ocean, a distance of twenty-five miles. There is also abundance of lake fish, varying in kind according to the season, which affords constant employment for fishermen who have no other occupation. Thanks to the refuse from the city, these fish are plump and tasty. Seeing the quantity on sale, you would imagine they could never be disposed of. But in a few hours the whole lot has been cleared away—so vast are the numbers of those accustomed to dainty living, to the point of eating fish and meat at one meal'.

At the Cat Bridge, Wei-the-Big-Knife offered his renowned cooked pork. The Chinese were, and are, great lovers of pork. Hundreds of pigs were slaughtered daily between 1 a.m. and dawn at the principal pork market off the Imperial Way and there were many pork-butchers' shops in the city which did their own butchering. Noodle merchants needed pork to add zest to their dishes. Pickled-pork merchants could hardly have done without it. Some taverns sold pork pies with their drinks, and street vendors offered fresh roast pork to hungry passers-by. Although Marco Polo said that there was always, in the ten principal markets of Hangchow (then called Kinsai), 'an abundance of victuals, both wild game such as roebuck, stags, harts, hares, and rabbits, and of fowls, such as partridges, pheasants, francolins [another species of partridge], quails, hens, capons, and as many ducks and geese as can be told', yet it was pork that was the backbone of the Chinese cuisine.

Residents of Hangchow were gourmets as far as rice was concerned. Rich families had their own specially selected rice imported daily into the city. It is difficult for Westerners to appreciate the infinite variety of rice, because in the West the choice tends to be limited to plump absorbent rice and thin unabsorbent rice. Neither is particularly appealing except as a background for something else. But in Asia, the range is wide. China had pink rice, white rice, yellow rice, mature rice and winter rice, to mention only a few. Many of them had a quite individual, almost flower-like fragrance which lingered even after cooking, and the Chinese custom of serving rice and other foods all in separate bowls made it possible for fine rice to be savoured as it deserved to be.

Pork and rice were the mainstays of Chinese cooking, although the economical Chinese, like the French of later days, made use of every possible edible vegetable. But European travellers constantly exclaimed over the quality of many Chinese foodstuffs. Friar Odoric de Pordenone, in the fourteenth century, was dazzled by cheap ginger and plump geese. 'Here you can buy three hundred pounds of fresh ginger for less than a groat! The geese too are bigger and finer and cheaper than anywhere in the world. For one of them is as big as two of ours, and 'tis all white as milk. . . . And these geese are as fat as fat can be, yet one of them well dressed and seasoned you shall have there [in Canton] for less than a groat. And as it is with the geese, so also with the ducks and fowls; they are so big that you would think them perfectly marvellous.'

Residents of Hangchow ate three meals a day: one at dawn, one at noon and one at sunset, and during the course of these three meals consumed

19] A nineteenth-century Chinese painting; sieving and pounding rice in the traditional manner

roughly 37 oz of rice per head (rather less than the questionable 42 oz a day allocated to Indians by the *Arthasastra*). Almost three hundred tons a day had to be imported into Hangchow by river to meet the demand.

Three meals a day was not by any means the total intake of a Hangchow citizen. Indeed, the Chinese themselves lent credence to the modern Western theory that Chinese food is five-minute food by their inordinate fondness for between-meal snacks. The itinerant roast-pork seller was always sure of his market. Other pedlars sold tea and gossip. Others, still, the sweetmeats—marvellously shaped, deliciously aromatic—which were a favourite of children and adults alike. And no one passing the Five Span Pavilion could be expected to resist Chou-Number-Five's honey fritters.

On important occasions Chinese householders were inclined to call in professional caterers. Friar Odoric reported that, in Honan, 'there is a custom . . . that if anyone desire to give a great dinner or entertainment to his friends he goes to one of the hostels which are established for this very purpose, and

20] A Sung painting (twelfth/thirteenth century) of a sweetmeat vendor. His stall, which rests on a bamboo trestle, has covered jars and open dishes of candied fruits and tiny cakes. It is protected by a canopy and decorated with flowers in a ceramic vase

saith to the host thereof: "Make me a dinner for such a number of my friends, and I propose to expend such and such a sum upon it." Then the host does exactly as ordered, and the guests are better served than they would have been in the entertainer's own house.' Modern Western practice differs much more from the Chinese than it did even a hundred years ago. Today, each Western course consists of a single dish—take it or leave it. As late as Regency times, however, a 'course' meant a variety of dishes, all placed on the table at one time; each guest ate as much or as little of each dish as he wanted to. The Chinese follow the same principle, preferring a little of several dishes to a single helping of one dish. A really grand banquet in thirteenth-century China, therefore, might number forty fragrant dishes of stir-fried, grilled or roasted seafood and meat; the same number of fruits and sweetmeats; half that number of vegetable dishes; close on a dozen rice dishes, differently flavoured; up to thirty variations on pungent dried fish; endless

21] The Hangchow district produced Forest of Fragrance tea, Jewel tea, and White Clouds tea. As with all teas, careful drying of the leaves was of supreme importance

desserts; and a wide choice of refreshing drinks which performed the same function as the *sorbets* of French banquets—cooling the palate and reviving the appetite between courses.

The two universal drinks of China were rice wine (fifty-four different varieties were recorded in Hangchow in the thirteenth century) and tea which had come into fashion in the seventh or eighth century. But tea, unlike many other Chinese products which had filtered through to the West from the earliest days, was scarcely even to be heard of in Europe before the sixteenth century, and not to be drunk there until the late seventeenth. In 1550, Haji Muhammad reported on it to the Venetian geographer, Ramusio. Tea, he said, was 'commonly used and much esteemed'. The people of Cathay 'take of that herb whether dry or fresh, and boil it well in water. One or two cups of this decoction taken on an empty stomach removes fever, headache, stomach ache, pain in the side or in the joints, and it should be taken as hot as you can bear it. . . . And those people would gladly give a sack of rhubarb [much prized in Europe] for an ounce of *Chiai Catai*.'

Hangchow in the thirteenth century looked to Marco Polo like the rich and favoured capital of a rich and enlightened land. It was, of course, largely uncharacteristic of the country, where people acquired a taste for snakes, grasshoppers and rats because they had to, but called them 'brushwood eels', 'brushwood shrimps', and 'household deer'. Nor were the Mongols easy masters. By the middle of the fourteenth century, their spies were stationed everywhere. Citizens were forbidden to gather into groups. No weapons were allowed; even kitchen tools which might have been used as weapons were restricted. There seemed no way for the Chinese to organize an uprising because communication was so difficult. Legend has it, however, that the problem was overcome by the characteristic Chinese fondness for sweetmeats. The Mongols had not thought of forbidding the traditional exchange of moon cakes between friends at the mid-autumn festival. When the next festival came round, each moon cake had a square of transparent paper attached to it inscribed with a call to rebellion. The result was a midnight massacre of the overlords and the ultimate overthrow of the dynasty. Moon cakes have traditionally been adorned with little paper squares ever since.

Five

'See the innumerable vessels', wrote Petrarch in fourteenth-century Venice, 'which set forth from the Italian shore in the desolate winter, in the most variable and stormy spring, one turning its prow to the east, the other to the west; some carrying our wine to foam in British cups, our fruits to flatter the palates of the Scythians and, still more hard of credence, the wood of our forests to the Aegean and Achaian isles; some to Syria, to Armenia, to the Arabs and Persians, carrying oil and linen and saffron, and bringing back all their diverse goods to us.' Romantic though it may sound, it was an ill-balanced trade. Venice exported bulky goods to the east—timber, wool and manufactured articles—and brought back spices, cargoes as compact and almost as expensive as gold dust. At the end of the fourteenth century, three galleys a year went to the Levant, and the goods they took with them could not even begin to match the value of the two thousand bales of ginger and pepper they brought back. Although Friar Odoric had said—with some exaggeration, perhaps—that one could buy three hundred pounds of fresh ginger in China for less than a Venetian groat, by the time the ginger and pepper of Asia reached the hands of the Arab middlemen endless landing charges, import dues and transport costs had been paid. The Arabs, in turn, extracted a generous profit, and when the Venetians, Genoese and, later, Florentines shipped the spices to western Europe, they, too, exacted their share. It was small wonder that the spice cupboards of mediaeval Europe were kept under lock and key by the lady of the house.

Well over half the average Venetian cargo consisted of pepper and dried ginger. But there were cloves, too, and cinnamon, candied sugar and green ginger, sweetmeats, mace and cardamom, the latter known in Europe as 'grains of paradise'. It has been estimated that each Venetian fleet at the end of the fourteenth century brought back 400,000 lb of spices. By the end of the

22] A fourteenth-century European view of the pepper harvest in southern India

fifteenth century, Venice had twenty great galleys each capable of loading 250 tons of goods.

The Arab-Venetian monopoly became intolerable to the rest of Europe. Columbus was sent out to find another route to the Spice Islands, and discovered America instead. Vasco da Gama was more immediately successful. The Portuguese achievement in opening a sea route to the Indies soon made Portugal almost as unpopular as the Venetians. In 1523 a German commission complained that 'the king of Portugal, with spices under his control, has set . . . prices as he will, because at no manner of dearness will they rest unsold among the Germans'. Spice prices, in fact, were grossly inflated. Seven years earlier, said the commission, saffron had cost two and a half *gulden* and six *kreutzers*; now it was sold at five and a half *gulden* and fifteen *kreutzers*. 'The merchants, moreover, do not make everything dear at the same time. Now it may be saffron and cloves. One year pepper and ginger, another year nutmeg, and so on, to the intent that their advantage may not at once be apparent to people.'

In the Middle Ages spice prices—particularly that of pepper—ruled the markets of the world, and the trade in spices tends to overshadow the very considerable commerce in other commodities. In the thirteenth century, for example, caravans of forty thousand horse still made the journey to Venice to buy salt for Hungary, Croatia and eastern Germany. In 1372 a fleet of two hundred ships put in at Bordeaux to load wine for England. Sicily exported large quantities of grain, cheese, sugar, butter, tuna and saltpetre to Italy, Provence and Catalonia. Flanders kept the cooking-pots of Europe stocked with onions. Crete and Corinth supplied England and Italy with thousands of gallons of Malmsey. France sent cheese and almonds to Italy, and Italy also imported rice from Spain. Raisins, prunes and dates reached northern Europe from the Levant and Portugal, and wine, oil and figs came from Chios, which was on the Genoese route from the east.

Merchants congregated at Venice for the great Christmas fairs, when the products of east and west were bought and sold. Conspicuous among the shipping in the harbour were the Flanders galleys, much of whose profit came from transporting exotic cargoes from the south to northern Europe. The trade of the Baltic and the North Sea was dominated first by the German Hanse towns and then by the Dutch, and the usual cargoes were commonplace necessities like timber, cloth, coal and metal, corn and fish. Fish, however, was a profitable business in Catholic Europe. Salt fish and 'stockfish' were the two major branches of the trade. Saltfishmongers handled salted and pickled herrings, whiting and mackerel, eels and cod, from the east coast of England, Holland and the Baltic. Stockfishmongers were merchants of dried fish, haddock, cod, pollack and ling, mainly from Iceland and Norway. The name 'stockfish' does not derive, tempting though the idea may be, from any suggestion that dried fish was useful for keeping in stock, but from the method of drying. In the fishing ports of Norway, the cod was hung to dry on thousands of racks made of sticks or *stokks*, from which the Norwegian name *stokk-fisk* comes. When the fish were simply laid on the rocks to dry, they were known as *klipp-fisk*.

The trade routes carried more than luxuries, food and raw materials, however. In the fourteenth century they also carried the Black Death, which spread from the Crimea in 1346 to Constantinople, Italy, western Europe, and finally (in 1350) to the North Sea and the Baltic countries. The population of Europe was consistently decimated by typhus, dysentery, diphtheria,

23] Lübeck, one of the Hanseatic towns whose prosperity was built on the Baltic trade

LVBEC.

LVBECA VRBS IMPERIALIS LIBERA, CIVITATVM WAN:
DALICARVM, ET INCLYTÆ HANSEATICÆ SOCIETATIS CAPVT.

leprosy and ergotism, but these killers were nothing in comparison with the Black Death. It is estimated that the population of Britain was halved in eighteen months, and that the mortality rate in other areas struck by the plague was as high as one person in three. In economic terms, this meant shortage of labour, the collapse of the manorial system, a reduction in community wealth, and an almost crippling blow to the economic growth rate. Yet, for a while at least, individual members of society were better off than they had been before, and the poor were certainly better fed than they were to be in the glorious and enlightened century of the Reformation, of Bluff King Hal and Good Queen Bess.

The European peasant never had a varied diet at any time in history. In good times there might be meat or fish almost every day—beef, mutton or veal, goose, an occasional fowl or rabbit; dried cod, salted herring or whale-meat during Lent and on fast days. When wall fires and chimneys were introduced in the fourteenth century, it became possible for the peasant to smoke his own bacon flitch in a grated recess in the chimney corner. There was bread and pease pottage, too, as well as milk, cheese and eggs. In warm southern Europe, where roast and boiled meat were less common, Italians retained the old Roman fondness for sausages and blood-puddings and had discovered *pasta*—derived, some say, from the descriptions of noodles brought back by enthusiastic travellers in China. The Mediterranean peoples, too, were less nervous of fruit than those in the north, and the habit of salads was not restricted only to the rich.

Discounting the periods when the peasant could find nothing to eat but bread, peas, beans and stolen game, what the historian refers to as a 'restricted' diet compares quite favourably with the diet of very many north Europeans today. Study the peasant foods of the Middle Ages, and then consider how many twentieth-century households rely on bread, frozen peas, beef, lamb, bacon, potatoes, eggs, sausages, and fish and chips. The peasant of the Middle Ages might not always be able to afford to kill a chicken or buy pike or sole on fish-days. But how often can the modern English housewife afford veal, home-produced lamb, or Scotch beef? There were undoubtedly spells of acute scarcity in the Middle Ages. Yet every European over the age of thirty-five today can remember the tiny pats of butter and sad fragments of meat which were accounted food for well over ten years during and after the Second World War. Indeed, the pease pottage of the Middle Ages was probably much more palatable than the oatmeal-and-cheese 'soup' and the luncheon-meat fritters of the 1940s. As always, language must be comparative. The peasant of the

Middle Ages *did* have a restricted diet in comparison with the diet of the rich and the bourgeoisie, who ate an astonishing variety of foods—including heron, crane and crow—with apparent gusto. The contrast today is less pronounced, largely because the rich customarily eat far fewer kinds of food than they used to. Gourmets may still feast on lampreys, on larks and blackbirds and figpeckers, on snails, frogs' legs, and even bird's-nest soup. But not everywhere, and not often.

24] A village under the snow.
Peasant life in fifteenth-century France

Nevertheless, bad times in the Middle Ages were very bad indeed. The twelfth century saw five long and terrible famines in Germany; in the thirteenth, England suffered from great scarcity; in the fourteenth, there were peasant revolts in England and France, neither of them primarily concerned with food shortages but both stimulated by fear of the possibility; and in the sixteenth century, the prospect of famine once again haunted Europe. In Tudor England, enclosures of land for grazing, as well as economic difficulties stemming from rather more complex origins, led to increased rents and prices and a time of hunger for the peasant. In France, it was reported that people in some areas were reduced to making bread from acorn flour, as they had done in the Dark Ages. Charles IX even went so far as to order vines to be rooted up to make way for corn, although his edict was soon repealed by Henri III. In the German territories, the end of the fifteenth century had been a good time. 'There was meat and food in plenty every day, and at fairs

and other frolics the tables almost broke with what they bore', recorded
Heinrich Müller. In Saxony a day labourer might earn sixteen *groschen* a week;
a good fat hen cost only half a *groschen*, a whole sheep or twenty-five codfish
four *groschen*, a bushel of rye six or seven *groschen*. But by the Reformation,
a little over twenty years later, wages had scarcely risen at all while rye had
gone up to twenty-five *groschen* a bushel, and a sheep to eighteen. Nor did
political factors help to ease the situation, for this was the century of atrocities
in Hungary, the peasant revolt and the white terror in Germany—when
Luther, the great reformer, claimed that 'whosoever may be killed on the side
of the authorities is a real martyr before God. . . . But whoever of the
peasantry perishes is of the eternal brood of hell'—and of Alva's terror in
the Low Countries.

  Throughout most of Europe it was the rulers' constant concern to ensure
basic supplies of corn, to equalize distribution of all foodstuffs, and to prevent
profiteering. Little could be done along these lines in the countryside, but the
authorities exercised rigid control over the markets in large towns. The
regulations made in 1345 for the sale of poultry in London are characteristic:

'Whereas heretofore folks bringing poultry to the City have sold their poultry
in lanes, in the hostels of their hosts, and elsewhere in secret, to the great loss
and grievance of the citizens, and at extortionate prices, and to the enhance-

25] London's Gracechurch market; those who came from out of town to sell their produce set up their stalls in the area
allocated to the county they came from

ment of the said poultry—we do command on behalf of our Lord the King that all strange folks bringing poultry to the City shall bring the same to the Leaden Hall and there sell it, and nowhere else; on pain of forfeiting the poultry and going bodily to prison, there at the discretion of the Mayor and Aldermen to remain.

'Also—that no person resident in the City who sells poultry shall be so daring as to come to the Leaden Hall, to sell or buy poultry there among the strangers, on pain of imprisonment; but let such persons sell their poultry at the stalls [in the street known as the Poultry] as of old they were wont to do. . . .

'Also—that all foreign [out-of-town] poulterers bringing poultry to the City should take it to the Leaden Hall and sell it there between Matins and the hour of Prime [midnight and 6 a.m.] to the reputable men of the City and their servants, for their own eating; and after the hour of Prime, the rest of their poultry that should remain unsold they might sell to [professional] cooks, regratresses [retailers], and such other persons as they might please.'

By controlling the place of sale, it was possible to some extent to control the quality of what was sold. The early archives of the City of London are studded with cases brought against dishonest food-sellers. Whether the comparative frequency of such trials indicates that there was a great deal of bad food sold in London in the fourteenth century is a matter for conjecture. It may simply mean that the authorities were wide awake enough to catch most of the offenders. One of the more attractive aspects of mediaeval justice was the custom of making the punishment fit the crime. In 1348, one John, son of John Gylessone, was accused of having 'exposed for sale in divers places in the City of London putrid and stinking meat; in deceit and to the peril of their lives of the persons buying the same, and to the scandal and disgrace of the Mayor, Aldermen, Sheriffs, and all the Commonalty of the city aforesaid'. The erring tradesman admitted that 'he had found a certain dead sow, thrown out near the ditch without Alegate, in the suburb of London; which sow he then flayed, and the flesh of the same, cooked as well as raw, he exposed for sale'. It was decreed that some of the flesh 'and the skin of the said sow, found in the possession of the said John, should be carried by the Sheriffs of the City in public before him, the said John, to the pillory on Cornhulle; and that he, the said John, should be first upon the pillory there, and the said flesh be burnt beneath him, while upon the pillory'.

Pork was a frequent headache to legislators, whether on the butcher's slab or on the hoof. In the twelfth century, half the householders of Paris kept pigs which roamed the streets in search of provender. As unofficial refuse collectors, they were invaluable, but they tended to trip up pedestrians and tangle up traffic. After the heir to the throne had fractured his skull when a pig ran between his horse's legs, an edict was issued that there should be no more pig-rearing in towns. Little attention seems to have been paid, however —or perhaps the custom waned and then increased again—for in the time of François I, four centuries later, the executioner was empowered to capture all the stray pigs he could find and take them to the Hôtel Dieu for slaughter. London suffered from the same nuisance, and in 1292 four men were sworn in as 'killers of swine' with the task of capturing and slaughtering 'such swine as should be found wandering in the King's highway, to whomsoever they might belong, within the walls of the City and the suburbs thereof'. In such cities as Frankfurt and Nuremberg, it was the custom to keep not only pigs, but sheep, cows and fowls as well. There, curiously enough, it was the pigsties rather than the pigs which were regarded as a nuisance, and in 1481 the Rath of Frankfurt was compelled to rule that pigsties should no longer be located in front of houses on the public street.

The banning of pigs in towns must have been a genuine deprivation, because pork has always been the most versatile of meats. Now, if the honest burgher wanted a fresh pork chop or a handsome roast leg, he had to buy it from the 'shambles', as the city's meat markets were called. There, meat was brought in on the hoof and slaughtered as and when required. But a pig bought from the shambles was a great deal more expensive than a home-reared pig, and not nearly as good. It had probably walked a long way to the slaughterhouse. And though the men of the Middle Ages did not know that it has an adverse effect on the meat when an animal is slaughtered in a fatigued or frightened state, they *did* know that pork from the shambles was tougher and turned rancid more quickly than home-killed pork. When the shambles were moved out of town, the problem of tainted meat increased. The Elizabethan housewife often dealt with superficial tainting (as the modern one does) by wiping meat with vinegar and relying on the heat of cooking to do the rest. But to the earlier, mediaeval mind, the smell of rancidity was an indication of pure poison. The people of the Middle Ages had grasped the principle of air-borne infection, but they believed that it was bad smells which transmitted it. This is one of the reasons why 'stinking and putrid' meat and fish were regarded with what nowadays appears to be disproportionate horror. It is also why, in 1306, the burning of coal was made a heavily punishable offence in London: the 'stench' was supposed to be unhealthy as well as disagreeable.

As fresh meat became more suspect, the townsman began to rely more and more on bacon and salt pork. In Paris, towards the end of Lent, there was a great ham fair. Everyone flocked to it to buy the hams, sausages and blood-puddings which formed the major part of the great end-of-Lent feast on Easter Day. According to the whims of the Church, dairy products were sometimes forbidden during Lent, and after forty days of no meat, no butter for cooking, no eggs, no milk, the population of Paris had a great deal to make up for. They did so with a banquet of all they liked best.

Retailers of ready-cooked meats had made an early appearance in many of the large towns of Europe, partly because few houses were adequately equipped for cooking. In London, towards the end of the twelfth century, William Fitzstephen described the advantages of the public cookshop which had been established on the banks of the Thames, where 'according to the season, you may find viands, dishes roast, fried and boiled, fish great and small, the coarser flesh for the poor, the more delicate for the rich, such as venison, and birds both big and little. If friends, weary with travel, should of a sudden come to any of the citizens, and it is not their pleasure to wait fasting till fresh food is bought and cooked . . . they hasten to the river bank, and there all things desirable are ready to their hand. . . . Those who desire to fare delicately need not search to find sturgeon or guinea-fowl or Ionian francolin, since all the dainties that are found there are set forth before their eyes. Now this is a public cookshop, appropriate to a city and pertaining to the art of civic life.' In 1363 a shoulder or leg of roast mutton cost $2\frac{1}{2}d$, and a capon baked in a pasty or a roast goose was sold at $7d$. Fifteen years later, prices had changed little. A roast goose still cost $7d$, but 'best capon baked in a pasty' had gone up to $8d$. A whole roast pig was to be had for $8d$, three roast pigeons for $2\frac{1}{2}d$, and ten roast finches for $1d$. Customers could have their own capons baked in a pasty if they paid $1\frac{1}{2}d$ for 'the paste, fire and trouble'.

In thirteenth-century Paris a housewife could buy ready-made pork, poultry or eel pasties, seasoned with pepper, as well as tarts and flans filled with soft cheese and fresh eggs. In 1557 the Venetian ambassador accredited to Paris commented on the ease with which one could buy all kinds of foods, either cooked or ready for the oven. He said that, to begin with, he had found it incredible that 'a capon, a partridge, a hare cost less ready to eat, larded and roasted, than if bought live in the market or the suburbs of Paris. This arises from the fact that the cookshops take them in bulk and have them at a low

26] A butcher's shop in the Low Countries. The diners in the cookshop or tavern attached appear
undismayed by the close proximity of a flayed ox

price.' The general price of food, however, was rather high, 'for the French
spend money on nothing as willingly as on food and what they call good
cheer. This is why butchers, meat-sellers, cookshops, retailers, pastry-cooks,
publicans and taverners are so numerous that there is real confusion; there is
no street so insignificant that they are not to be found there.' For centuries,
there had even been street vendors who sold the housewife whatever she
needed, including ready-made sauces—'yellow sauce', in which ginger and
saffron predominated; 'green sauce', of ginger, cloves, cardamom and green
herbs; and the fourteenth-century favourite, cameline. There was summer
cameline and winter cameline. The Goodman of Paris, who wrote a household
hints manuscript for his youthful wife, favoured the following recipe. 'Break
ginger, cinnamon and saffron and half a nutmeg moistened with wine, then
take it out of the mortar. Then have white breadcrumbs, not toasted but
moistened in cold water, and broken in the mortar. Moisten them with wine
and sieve them. Then boil all together and put in brown sugar last of all; and
that is winter cameline.' It was to be served with poultry or game birds.

Fish, an important part of the mediaeval diet, was carefully controlled.
Thames fishermen were prosecuted for using small-mesh nets; the mesh was
supposed to be wide enough to allow small fry to slip through. The fishermen
of the Seine were expected to throw small fish back in the water, and all fish

27] Fish was brought to Paris in ventilated barges or barrels

was inspected officially before being put on sale. In Venice, the fishermen's catch had to be brought to the Tall Pole at San Marco or the Rialto, to be valued, pay duty, and be sold. The fishmarkets were inspected daily, and all suspect fish destroyed. Equally stringent regulations were applied to other foodstuffs in Venice—notably pork, wine, oil and drugs. An unusually colourful violation cropped up in 1498 when certain cooking-oil vendors were caught selling oil in which syphilis patients had been immersed for an attempted cure. The oil was found to be full of 'impurities and organisms'!

It was hardly surprising that the Middle Ages suffered from so many ailments. The authorities tried to impose basic laws of hygiene, but their attempts were constantly frustrated. One of the great sources of annoyance was the slaughter of meat in cities, and in 1369 'Edward, by the grace of God' informed the mayor, recorder, aldermen and sheriffs of his capital city of London that he had received 'grievous complaint' from the citizens who lived near the slaughterhouse of St Nicholas.

'We had heard that by reason of the slaughtering of beasts in the said shambles, and the carrying of the entrails and offal of the said beasts through the streets, lanes and places aforesaid to the said banks of the river, at a place called "Butchersbridge", where the same entrails and offal are thrown into the water aforesaid, and the dropping of the blood of such beasts between the said shambles and the waterside aforesaid—the same running along the midst of the said streets and lanes—grievous corruption and filth have been generated, as well in the water as in the streets, lanes and places aforesaid, and the parts adjacent in the said city; so that no one, by reason of such corruption and filth, could hardly venture to abide in his house there. And we, considering the damages, grievances and evils which, from carrying the entrails and offal of the beasts so in the said shambles slaughtered to the water aforesaid, by reason of the corruption and grievous stenches and abominable sights . . . determined with the assent of all our Parliament aforesaid that the said bridge should, before the Feast of St Peter's Chains [1 August] last past, be pulled down and wholly removed; it being our desire that such slaughtering of beasts should be done without the city.'

The mayor, recorder, aldermen and sheriffs had apparently failed to have the bridge demolished by the Feast of St Peter's Chains, and the king suggested that they would be well advised to get it done by the forthcoming Feast of

28] A flock of sheep and a pig are driven to the shambles in Paris

the Assumption of the Blessed Virgin Mary (15 August). Two years later, however, the shambles of St Nicholas were still causing 'abominations and stenches' by throwing 'blood and entrails' into the streets and the Thames, and the king was still threatening both the butchers and the civic dignitaries with dire retribution.

In Paris, half a century later, 'Charles, by the grace of God' was having much the same kind of trouble. 'We have commanded, and we command, so that the air of our said city be not infected nor corrupted by these slaughterhouses and knackers' yards, and also that the water of the river Seine be not corrupted nor infected by the blood and other filth of the said beasts falling or being thrown into the said river Seine, that all slaughterhouses and knackers' yards establish themselves outside our said city of Paris. . . .'

But of all man's foods, bread was the most important. The finest bread—eaten by the rich in the early days, and demanded by every citizen as the centuries progressed—was known in England as manchet. It was made from fine wheat flour from which most of the bran particles had been sieved out. Chet bread was coarser, containing more of the bran, and there were other flours coarser still. It was not unknown for really coarse flour to contain chips of grinding stone as well as bran. The commonest flour, perhaps, between the fourteenth and seventeenth centuries, was that known as maslin (or, in France, *miscelin*, *rousset*, or *métail*). This was made from a mixed crop of wheat and rye.

Different flours had different characteristics. These were precisely specified by the Yorkshire squire, Henry Best, who stored grain for home use as follows:

'For brown bread. Rye, pease, barley in equal quantities. In summer less barley.

'For the folks' puddings. Barley. . . . Never use any rye for puddings, because it maketh them so soft that they run about the platters.

'For our bread and for the folks' piecrusts. Maslin. . . . The folks' pie-crusts are made of maslin, as our bread is, because paste that is made of barley meal cracketh and splitteth.

'For our own pies. Best wheat.'

By feudal law, the lord of the manor was compelled to bake his tenants' bread, and the tenant was taxed for the privilege. In some countries, during the early Middle Ages, the law was interpreted in such a way that the peasant was forbidden to grind his own flour or bake his own bread. Grinding flour at home in a hand-mill was not a particularly pleasant task, but it was still preferable to tramping miles over muddy paths only to find that the miller's pool had run dry. The monopolistic miller could afford to be as surly and thievish as he chose, and the peasant often had to accept ill-ground grain and flour invisibly diluted with sand. Chaucer's Miller was characteristic of the breed—'Well could he stealen corn, and take toll thrice.'

Bakers were regarded as superior to millers—in Germany the murderer of a baker was liable to three times the fine imposed on any other murderer—but they were just as dishonest. In 1327, one John Brid, a London baker,

'did skilfully and artfully cause a certain hole to be made upon a table of his, called a "moulding-board", pertaining to his bakehouse, after the manner of a mousetrap, in which mice are caught; there being a certain wicket warily provided for closing and opening such hole.

'And when his neighbours and others who were wont to bake their bread at his oven came with their dough or material for making bread, the said John used to put such dough or other material upon the said table, called a "moulding-board", as aforesaid, and over the hole before-mentioned. . . . The same John had one of his household, ready provided for the same, sitting in secret beneath such table; which servant of his, so seated beneath the hole and carefully opening, it, piecemeal and bit by bit craftily withdrew some of the dough aforesaid, frequently collecting great quantities from such dough, falsely, wickedly and maliciously; to the great loss of all his neighbours and persons living near, and of others who had come to him with such dough to bake.'

With the stolen dough, John Brid and the many other bakers who used the same trick made bread for public sale. The Bread Assize (*Assisa Panis*) of 1266 had fixed the weight of various types of loaf in relation to cost, and one of the most common (and frequently detected) crimes was selling short-weight bread. In the early years of the fourteenth century, the halfpenny loaf of maslin bread was supposed to weigh twenty-eight shillings (the shilling, $\frac{3}{5}$ oz, was used as a standard measure, as were other coins), and the halfpenny loaf of wastel bread, a coarse bread, forty-two shillings. Bakers who were found guilty of contravening the weight laws were drawn through the city streets on a hurdle, with the offending loaf hung round their necks. Those who stole their customers' dough, however, were condemned to the pillory.

29] A dishonest baker, with an underweight loaf tied round his neck, is dragged through London's dirtiest streets on a hurdle

In France, there was also price-control of bread. When corn cost six *gros*, the one-*denier* white loaf was supposed to weigh five *ouches* and ten *estrelins*, and the brown seven *ouches* and six *estrelins*. But when corn went up to twenty-four *gros*, the weight of the loaves was reduced to three *ouches* fifteen *estrelins* and five *ouches* respectively. Every week in Paris, inspectors seized underweight loaves from bakers, as well as overbaked and otherwise faulty bread. The bread which had been seized in the suburbs was put up for sale to the poor each Sunday at the market outside Notre Dame. Loaves which had been confiscated for the same reasons in Paris itself were distributed free to the needy.

It seems fairly clear that, although raised bread had been known since the days of ancient Egypt, it was by no means universal in the Middle Ages. Though Paris bakers used yeast for pastries, they rarely used it for bread before the sixteenth century. This is not as strange as it may seem. Bread fulfilled three functions in the cuisine of the Middle Ages. It was extensively used for thickening sauces. It was used instead of plates in the majority of households. And it was used, as it is today, for filling up empty corners of the stomach. In the first case, unleavened bread was perfectly adequate. In the second case, unleavened was better than leavened bread.

This is, perhaps, the place to describe the trencher, or bread platter, used during the whole of the Middle Ages. Whatever was to be eaten at a meal was served up on the table in serving dishes made of wood, sometimes of earthenware or pewter, or possibly of precious metal in a royal or baronial household. If only husband and wife were seated at table, they had no need of platters

30] When John I of Portugal entertained John of Gaunt, they ate (according to the artist) from bread trenchers. A pile of reserve trenchers can be seen to the right of the serving-hatch

but simply ate straight from the serving dish. Where there were more diners, however, it was the custom for each to have before him one or more thick slices (about six inches across by two or three deep) of two-day-old bread to which he transferred food from the serving dish, or on which the carver placed slices of roast meat. Since so many mediaeval dishes consisted of minced meat or meat chunks in thick sauce, the trencher easily became saturated even when it was made of heavy, unleavened bread. If porous leavened bread had been used, the sauce would have soaked through even more rapidly.

The third function of bread, as a filler, was of less importance. In rich households, certainly, separate fine-quality bread was eaten with meals. But in most homes the family simply ate the trencher after the main part of the meal was over, as Indians ate their *chapatis*. It was a very economical system.

Although French bakers sold little raised bread, well-to-do households probably made their own. Home-made bread was cooked in various ways. Some cooks took their dough to the bake-house to be baked for them. Others had their own egg-shaped baking ovens, which were heated by filling with charcoal or embers, raked out before the bread was put in. The poorer household contented itself with 'ashcakes'—known in France as *fouaces* or *fougasses* (from the Latin *focus*, hearth)—which were laid on the hearth to cook, and covered with an earthenware or iron pan round which hot embers were raked. In Scotland, where bread ovens were unknown until the middle of the eighteenth century, flat cakes and bannocks were cooked on an iron griddle over the fire.

31] A fifteenth-century bakehouse

What did the people of the Middle Ages eat with their bread? In the case of the rich, the succinct answer is 'too much'. Among the literary relics of the period is a French morality play entitled *The Condemnation of Banquet*. In the play, Banquet, Dinner and Supper are personified as three villainous poisoners who lead astray a band of rattlepates named Gluttony, Tit-bit, I-drink-with-you, and so on. Ultimately the poisoners are brought before the tribunal of Dame Experience. Banquet is condemned out of hand, but Dinner and Supper, being indispensable, are allowed to live—with the proviso that they reside six hours apart.

Nowadays, at even the most magnificent banquet, a guest is unlikely to have more than one plate of hors d'œuvre, one soup, one fish dish, one meat dish, vegetables, salad, savoury or cheese, and a sweet. In the Middle Ages and after, everyone ate—so to speak—*à la carte*. All the alternatives for each course were set on the table at one time, and the temptation to sample several dishes was irresistible.

Nor were courses as clearly defined as they are today. There was nothing in the least unusual about a 'course' which offered meat, soup, and poultry, in a variety of different ways. Take, for example, a sixteenth-century banquet on the grand scale, served at the table of Pope Pius V.

FIRST COURSE. COLD DELICACIES FROM THE SIDEBOARD

Pieces of marzipan and marzipan balls
Neapolitan spice cakes
Malaga wine and Pisan biscuits
Plain puff pastries made with milk and eggs
Fresh grapes
Spanish olives
Prosciutto cooked in wine, sliced and served with capers, grape pulp and sugar
Salted pork tongues cooked in wine, sliced
Spit-roasted songbirds, cold, with their tongues sliced over them
Sweet mustard

SECOND COURSE. HOT FOODS FROM THE KITCHEN, ROASTS

Fried veal sweetbreads and liver, with a sauce of aubergines, salt, sugar and pepper
Spit-roasted skylarks with lemon sauce
Spit-roasted quails with sliced aubergines
Stuffed spit-roasted pigeons with sugar and capers sprinkled over them
Spit-roasted rabbits, with sauce and crushed pine nuts
Partridges larded and spit-roasted, served with lemon slices
Puff pastries filled with minced veal sweetbreads and served with slices of prosciutto
Heavily seasoned poultry with lemon slices and sugar
Slices of veal, spit-roasted, with a sauce made from the juices
Leg of goat, spit-roasted, with a sauce made from the juices
Soup of almond paste, with the flesh of three pigeons to each serving
Squares of meat aspic

32] A rich Italian kitchen of the late Renaissance. Running water appears to be connected to the fish tank, and a cauldron rests on brick supports over the fire. In the foreground, pasta-making is in progress

THIRD COURSE. HOT FOODS FROM THE KITCHEN, BOILED MEATS AND STEWS

Stuffed fat geese, boiled Lombard style and covered with sliced almonds, served with cheese, sugar and cinnamon

Stuffed breast of veal, boiled, garnished with flowers

Very young calf, boiled, garnished with parsley

Almonds in garlic sauce

Turkish-style rice with milk, sprinkled with sugar and cinnamon

Stewed pigeons with mortadella sausage and whole onions

Cabbage soup with sausages

Poultry pie, two chickens to each pie

Fricasseed breast of goat dressed with fried onions

Pies filled with custard cream

Boiled calves' feet with cheese and egg

33] The mansions of the rich usually had dove or pigeon cotes to supply the table during winter. Some even had extensive poultry yards where fowls, ducks and other birds could be raised. The peacock in Jan Steen's painting was probably destined to be served up, in full plumage, at a banquet

FOURTH COURSE. DELICACIES FROM THE SIDEBOARD
Bean tarts
Quince pastries, one quince per pastry
Pear tarts, the pears wrapped in marzipan
Parmesan cheese and Riviera cheese
Fresh almonds on vine leaves
Chestnuts roasted over the coals and served with salt, sugar and pepper
Milk curds with sugar sprinkled over
Ring-shaped cakes
Wafers made from ground corn

After the fourth course, the table was cleared, hands were washed in scented water, clean napkins were provided, and stalks of sweet fresh fennel, bunches of scented flowers, toothpicks in dishes of rosewater, and sweets and confections were placed on the board.

Although grand, the papal menu on this occasion was comparatively restrained and even a weak modern stomach might have faced it—except, perhaps, for the third course. Less elevated hosts tended to be more pretentious. In 1532, for example, Grimani gave a banquet to Farnese in Venice. The dinner lasted for four hours; there were one hundred guests and ninety different dishes. Echoing the great days of Rome, Grimani's chef provided pasties at the end of the feast; when the pasties were cut, out flew a number of birds, and there was great confusion as the guests scrambled to catch them. The recipe for such pasties had, in fact, been published in an Italian cookery book some years earlier.

TO MAKE PIES THAT THE BIRDS MAY BE ALIVE IN THEM, AND FLY OUT WHEN IT IS CUT UP

Make the coffin [piecrust] of a great pie or pasty. In the bottom thereof make a hole as big as your fist, or bigger if you will. Let the sides of the coffin be somewhat higher than ordinary pies. Which done, put it full of flour and bake it, and being baked, open the hole in the bottom and take out the flour. Then, having a pie of the bigness of the hole in the bottom of the coffin aforesaid, you shall put it into the coffin, withal put into the said coffin round about the aforesaid pie as many small live birds as the empty coffin will hold, besides the [small] pie aforesaid. And this is to be done at such time as you send the pie to the table, and set before the guests: where, uncovering or cutting up the great lid of the pie, all the birds will fly out, which is to delight and pleasure show to the company. And that they be not altogether mocked, you shall cut open the small pie.

Certainly, it *sounds* simple enough.

Renaissance chefs were not in the least dismayed when they were expected to produce great banquets on fish days. When Elisabeth of Austria made her ceremonial entry into Paris in 1571, one of her first duties was to attend mass at Notre Dame and dine thereafter in the hall of the bishopric. There, since it was a Friday, she was served with:

Four large fresh salmon	Fifty crabs
Ten large turbots	Eighteen trout, a foot and a half
Eighteen brill	long
Eighteen 'grenaulx' [fish resembling	Nine large pike, two to three
large gurnet]	feet long

Eighteen mullet

Three creels of large smelts

Two creels of oysters in their shells

Two hundred cod tripes

Fifty pounds of whale [probably the salted blubber]

One creel of oysters without shells

Two hundred white herrings

Two hundred red herrings

Twenty-four cuts of salted salmon

Twelve lobsters

Nine fresh shad

Twelve large carp, two to three feet long

Fifty one-foot carp

Eight one-foot pike

Eighteen lampreys

Two hundred fat young lampreys

Two hundred fat crayfish

One creel of mussels

One thousand frogs [which were regarded as marine animals rather than flesh]

The variety of fish is impressive, to say the least—all the more so since the dinner was given at the end of March, not the best season for any food. The purveyor, however, had found himself unable to supply sturgeon, dorado, porpoise, turtle and fresh mackerel, all of which had been requested by the queen's Parisian hosts.

At much the same time, the economist Jean Bodin was complaining: 'No one is content at any ordinary dinner with having three courses, the first of boiled meats, the second of roast, and the third of fruit. Meat must appear in five or six different ways, with so many sauces, minces, pastries, so many salmagundis of all kinds, and other varieties of mishmash, that there is great dissipation.' Bodin suggested that the economy would be better off and the people healthier if they reverted to what he called 'old-fashioned frugality', making do with only five or six different kinds of meat, plainly cooked.

Sumptuary laws were, in fact, in force at the time. Edicts of 1563, 1565, 1566, 1567, 1572 and 1577 all tried to impose some restraint on the Parisian passion for food. Even at festivals, three courses was supposed to be the maximum. The entrées were not to consist of more than six dishes of soup, fricassee or pastries. The meat or fish course was limited also to six dishes, and no doubling up was allowed—in other words, if one of the dishes was capon, it was to contain one capon only, not two. Nor were meat and fish to be served at the same meal. The dessert might consist of fruits, tarts, pasties and cheese, but not more than six varieties. A host who contravened these edicts was liable to a heavy fine. And not only the host. His guests were fined, too, and the unfortunate cook who provided the meal was sent to prison for fifteen days on bread and water.

34] Veronese's painting *The Marriage at Cana* originally decorated the refectory of a Benedictine monastery in Venice. Appropriately enough, he was paid for it not only in money but in food and wine. Despite the title, the banquet represents one of those typically Renaissance occasions which the sumptuary laws were designed to control

In Venice, too, sumptuary laws were in force. In 1460 it had been ruled that one and a half ducats per head was the maximum that was to be spent on any banquet, and in 1512 servants and cooks in private houses were compelled to conduct police through the banqueting hall so that they might inspect the fare that was being offered. Pheasant, peacock, guinea-fowl, blackcock and woodcock were all banned, as were trout and other freshwater fish. In fifteenth-century Florence, three courses was the maximum permitted at dinner; two at supper. The cook had to inform a public official what he intended to serve.

Rulers, however, had been trying and failing to impose laws against extravagance for centuries. In ancient Rome, the Didian law of 143 BC had limited the number of guests and the amount of food at entertainments. In 1294, Philippe le Bel of France had restricted family meals to a mere two dishes plus soup for dinner. In 1363 Edward III of England had aimed his sumptuary legislation at the servant classes, who were developing ideas beyond their station—no doubt because of the servant shortage which was one of the results of the Black Death—when he attempted to control not only how much they ate but what they wore. Kings might command, but few people obeyed. Genuinely powerful monarchs are a historical rarity.

If the sumptuary laws had been regarded, vegetables might have found a more important place in the European diet. For many centuries, however, vegetables were largely disdained—except for the ubiquitous onions and cabbages. Certainly, herbs were grown in many garden plots. They were the poor man's spices and, in company with garlic, his medicine as well. Peas and broad beans, too, were grown, the first to be made into flour which could be mixed with rye or wheat flour for bread, or into sustaining pease-porridge and pease-pudding, the second mainly for winter cattle fodder. But although radishes, spinach, lettuce, parsnips, turnips, carrots and beets were known, they were rarities. This was particularly the case in England, although Alexander Neckam, abbot of Cirencester, claimed a surprisingly comprehensive list of plants in his garden at the beginning of the thirteenth century. On the basis of his own garden, he advised that noble gardens 'should be adorned with roses and lilies, turnsole [heliotrope], violets and mandrake; there you should have parsley and cost and fennel, and southernwood, and coriander, sage, savory, hyssop, mint, rue, dittany, smallage, pellitory, lettuce, garden cress, peonies. There should also be planted beds with onions, leeks, garlic, pumpkins and shallots; the cucumber growing in its lap, the drowsy poppy, the daffodil and brank-ursine [acanthus] ennoble a garden. There should also be pottage herbs, such as beets, herb-mercury, orach [mountain spinach], sorrel and mallows; anise, mustard, white pepper and wormwood do good service to the gardenlet.' The abbot went on to recommend medlars, quinces, warden [pear] trees, peaches, pomegranates, lemons, oranges, almonds, dates and figs. His list of fruit trees is certainly suspect, as lemons, oranges and dates in the thirteenth century were—as they are now—hot-climate crops. Possibly the abbot was filling out his own limited experiments with advice culled from a manuscript of the Mediterranean work, Palladius *On Husbandry*. Most of the vegetables and herbs he mentions, however, may very well have been grown in England. Some were used in salads and cooking, some (such as southernwood) were used for scattering among the rushes which carpeted mediaeval floors, to give a sweet smell and drive away fleas and other domestic pests. Roses were used to perfume the water in which dinner guests washed their hands before and after eating. And some, such as violets, were used medicinally as well as decoratively. According to a sixteenth-century herbal, 'the syrup of violets is good against the inflammation of the lungs and breast, and against the pleurisy, and cough, and also against fevers or agues, but especially in young children'. The root of the white lily, pounded with honey, was also accounted a cure for 'all manner of naughty scurviness'; boiled in vinegar, it was said to cause 'the corns which be in the feet to fall off if it be kept upon the said corns as a plaster by the space of three days without removing'.

Gardening in Flanders and Italy was much more advanced than in England or France. Indeed, English gardening only really began to look up when Flemish refugees from Alva's terror arrived in the country. By the end of the sixteenth century, there had been a considerable increase in vegetable growing. In France, the improvement began after 1533, when Catherine de Medici arrived from Florence to marry the dauphin, later Henri II. In her train came Italian cooks, who complained bitterly at the absence of the vegetables they were accustomed to in Italy. They—and the cooks of Marie de Medici, who came to France at the end of the century as the bride of Henri IV—introduced not only the renowned Italian cuisine into France, but such vegetables as artichokes, broccoli, savoy cabbages and *petit pois* as well.

Although vegetables do not figure largely in Italian banquet menus, one late fifteenth-century writer said that 'you would think all the gardens in the world were at Venice', such was the splendour and number of fruits and vegetables to be found in the Venetian markets. Physicians, still labouring under the doctrines of the Salerno school, attributed every conceivable disease to the Italians' fondness for such foods. In this, they were wide of the mark—in one direction at least. As modern dieticians have pointed out, the population of England must have existed in a state of scurvy, mild or acute, for many centuries, because of the almost total lack of vitamin C. The Italians' liking for fruit and salads must have guarded them fairly well against scurvy. On the other hand, it was not unreasonable for physicians to be wary of fruit. Fruit is a summer food, and summer—in an era when knowledge of hygiene was even sketchier than it is today—was the peak time for dysentery. Furthermore, fruit and green vegetables in large quantities do have a laxative effect, and Italians who could not afford a great deal of meat may well have eaten fruit and salads to excess, since it takes a great deal more of these to fill the stomach than it does of meat in thick sauces.

In the fourteenth century, the French treated vegetables even more harshly than the British have been accused of doing in more recent times. The

35] In *The Supper at Emmaus* Caravaggio painted a meal which, to the average Italian, appeared simple but perfect—bread, a chicken and a variety of fruits

Goodman of Paris recommended that his young wife treat Roman (or winter) cabbages thus: 'Know that cabbages require to be put on the fire very early in the morning and cooked for a very long time, much longer than any other pottage, and on a good, strong fire, and they should be diluted with beef fat and none other, whether they be hearts or early cabbages, or whatever they be save sprouts. Know also that the greasy pot-water of beef and mutton is proper thereto, but in no wise that of pork, which is only good for leeks.'

In 1375 the first cookery book of modern times appeared. It was compiled by Guillaume Tirel, 'first squire of the kitchen' to Charles VI of France and previously (at the time when the manuscript was written) cook to Charles V, for whose kitchen staff the book was intended. It was written under the pseudonym of Taillevent. Although in modern French *taille-vent* means seagull, it is very tempting to take the word in its literal sense of 'cut wind'—for the mediaeval digestive system was much afflicted by wind, and any author who offered the promise of reducing it would have been a popular man indeed. Unfortunately, the recipes in *Le Viandier*, as the book is known, hold out little hope. One of the banquets Taillevent served to the king began with capons in cinnamon sauce, chicken with herbs and spices, cabbage, and venison. Not—in view of the spices and cabbage—an auspicious beginning.

The cuisine of Charles VI is notable for more than a cookery book. It was reputedly Charles's queen, Isabeau of Bavaria, who introduced the written menu, so that guests might know what they were eating. In view of the lavishness with which the first squire of the royal kitchen used spices, a normal palate could hardly have been expected to identify the basic ingredients without some such aid.

A few years after Tirel produced his manual for the kitchen of the French king, a similar work appeared for the instruction of the cooks of Richard II of England. This was known as *The Forme of Cury* [*Cookery*] and had much in common with *Le Viandier*. Both books rely on heavy spicing, and most of the food is minced or chopped so that it may conveniently be eaten with a spoon. A major role is played by Blank Manng, the ancestor of the modern blanc-mange, which was a creamy almond mixture frequently added to meat dishes by way of sauce. Galantines and gruels are common to both books. Few of the dishes look appealing at first sight, but Richard II's salad offers a welcome reprieve. 'Take parsley, sage, garlic, chibollas [i.e. what are still called syboes in Scotland, shallots elsewhere], onions, leeks, borage, mints, fennel, and to them [add] cresses, rue, rosemary, purslane. Rinse, and wash them clean; pick them over, pluck them small with thine hands, and mix them well with raw oil. Lay on vinegar and salt and serve it forth.'

The first printed cookery book came, as was hardly surprising, from Renaissance Italy in 1475. It was written—and this, superficially, *was* surprising—by the Vatican librarian. Renaissance humanists, however, were interested in everything, even in the mundane subject of food which so many subsequent philosophers and historians have regarded as a matter of no importance. The librarian's name was Bartolomeo de Sacchi, but he was known as Platina. His book, *De Honesta Voluptate*, was partly a cookery book and partly a guide to good health. The recipes offered no really new departures, but they were much more precise than before and even went so far as to specify quantities. The main interest of Platina's book lies in its good sense. Eat well, he said, but pay attention to what you eat and when you eat—and don't quarrel on a full stomach.

Platina's injunction not to quarrel on a full stomach was aimed more at improving digestion than improving manners. But the various 'courtesy books' which appeared from the thirteenth century onwards had manners

36] Platina kneels before the Pope

very much in mind. 'If thou art eating with others', advised Fra Bonvicino da Riva in 1290, 'make no uproar or disturbance, even though thou shouldst have reason therefor. If any of thy companions should transgress', he added ominously, 'pass it by till the time comes.'

The courtesy books are irresistibly riddled with do's and don'ts. They give a hair-raising picture of table manners in the Middle Ages. To understand them, however, it is necessary to remember that the act of eating was then not the solitary act it is today. Men of the highest rank had their own dishes, but everyone else ate in pairs. Each diner had his trencher, but the food (except for individually carved roasts) was placed on the table in servings for two. This may not sound very important—but there were no serving spoons and forks, the dining fork was used nowhere but in Italy until the seventeenth century, and the customary eating tools were the fingers. Each diner fished with his fingers in the bowls which he shared with his neighbour, conveyed a portion of food to his trencher, and then to his mouth. The cleanliness of one's neighbour's fingers was therefore a matter for some concern.

A thirteenth-century German courtesy book, written by an Italian known as Thomasin von Zerclaere, contented itself with saying: 'A man who is well balanced in his mind, when he begins to eat, he touches nothing but his food with the hand.' Fra Bonvicino was more specific:

'Let thy hands be clean.
Thou must not put either thy fingers into thine ears, or thy hands
    on thy head.
The man who is eating must not be cleaning
By scraping with his fingers at any foul part.'

Probably, by 'any foul part', Fra Bonvicino meant spots or stains on the clothing. But sins such as these paled before the instructions of later writers, who enjoined their readers not to blow their noses with their fingers, and—please—not to go scraping and scratching at that part of the male anatomy which the Middle Ages and the Elizabethans called the 'codware'.

Scratching, in days when fleas and bugs were omnipresent, was one of the habits most inveighed against in the courtesy books, especially the habit of scratching with soupy fingers. 'You must not scratch your throat', said the fourteenth-century German, Tannhäuser, 'whilst you eat, with the bare hand. But if it happen that you cannot help scratching, then courteously take a portion of your dress, and scratch with that. That is more befitting than that your skin should become dirtied.'

Napkins do not appear to have been in common use in Tannhäuser's time, but, if Giovanni della Casa is any guide, the presence of napkins in sixteenth-century Italy had contributed little to cleanliness. After discussing gluttons who dipped their hands into the serving dishes almost to the elbow, he remarked that they made a fearful mess of their napkins. 'And these same napkins they will use to wipe off perspiration, and even to blow their noses. You must not so soil your fingers as to make the napkin nasty in wiping them; neither clean them upon the bread which you are to eat.' Della Casa's Victorian translator could not here restrain himself from interpolating: 'We should hope not!'

Cleanliness was by no means the only subject under discussion. Diners were told not to 'poke about everywhere, when thou hast meat, or eggs, or some such dish. He who turns and pokes about on the platter, searching, is unpleasant, and annoys his companion at dinner.' So said Fra Bonvicino. But Tannhäuser knew an even better way to offend fellow guests.

> Some people are inclined,
> When they have gnawed a bone,
> To put it back again into the dish.
> This you should consider as acting greatly amiss.

The floor was the place for such relics, even in the best-appointed household. When Benvenuto Cellini was a young man, his employer made 'a very large vase designed for the table of Pope Clement, into which at dinnertime were thrown bones and the rinds of fruits'. Perhaps the Pope, at least, preferred a boneless floor? But no. 'It was made', Benvenuto went on, 'rather for display than necessity.'

Meat, or fish, eaten during the Middle Ages can be divided into dishes of four different consistencies. There was roast meat, which was carved at table and served by the carver directly on to each guest's trencher. The guest then dipped each piece of meat into the sauce of his choice; these sauces were distributed around the table in, reasonably enough, saucers. As well as roast meat, there were meat stews of thick consistency, in which the meat had

37] By the end of a meal, the floor was a paradise for domestic pets

usually been left on the bone. Since it is hardly possible to eat, say, a leg of chicken with a spoon, it was this type of dish into which fingers were most frequently dipped. A third type of dish was the thin stew or thick soup of which frumenty was a popular example. It was made by boiling hulled wheat in milk and adding meat chunks, venison, or fish, as well as a variety of spices and seasonings. This was eaten, frequently with a spoon, direct from the serving dish, and it was considered bad manners for a guest to dip his spoon in the stew at the same time as his neighbour. Finally, there was a thinner soup which was drunk out of porringers in the same manner as out of cups.

Dishes of the frumenty type were a good indication of the host's meanness or generosity. The more pieces of meat—or 'sops'—they contained, the better. The French word *soupe* originally meant whatever was cooked in a liquid; the English 'sop' comes from this. Later *soupe* came to mean the liquid itself; and the English language adopted the word once more, this time as 'soup'. Shortage of sops was greatly frowned upon. In the early seventeenth century, for example, the Sieur de Vandy dined at the home of the Comte de Grandpré. 'They placed before him a soup in which there were only two poor sops chasing each other around. Vandy tried to take one up but, as the plate was enormous, he missed his aim; he tried again, and could not catch it. He rose from the table and called his valet de chambre.

'"You there! Pull off my boots."

'"What are you going to do?" his neighbour asked him.

'"Permit me to have my boots removed," said Vandy coldly, "and I propose to dive into that plate in order to seize that sop."'

A revolutionary dining aid, the fork, was relatively common among the Italian nobility from the fifteenth century onwards, but other nations were very slow to adopt it. The principle of the fork was not new; it had been known as a cooking implement for centuries. Various monarchs, too, had used small forks—often made of precious metal—for particular foods. The Dogaressa Selvo had availed herself of the idea as early as the eleventh

38] In 1523, a Venetian nobleman's table usually featured a fork (two-pronged) as well as a pointed knife

century. A fork was itemized in an inventory of the property of Edward I of England in 1297, and in that of Louis d'Anjou in 1368. Charles V of France had one in 1380, which he used for toasted cheese. The cheese, incidentally, was served sprinkled with sugar and powdered cinnamon. Other nobles used forks for eating comfits, or for fishing bread sops out of wine. But only the Italians used them as dining implements. In 1518 a French silk merchant, Jaques le Saige, attended a ducal banquet in Venice and approved the fact 'that these seigneurs, when they want to eat, take the meat up with a silver fork'. Yet even when Catherine de Medici went to France, the fork did not catch on there. Her favourite son, Henri III, did not adopt it until after he had visited Venice. His visit was noteworthy for another example of Italian ingenuity. He was entertained to a collation at which bread, plates, knives, forks, tablecloths and napkins were all made of spun sugar. It was a pretty conceit—and a practical joke, for the napkin broke in the king's hand.

Henri III approved the fork, and used it, but Louis XIV, a century later, still regarded it as a superfluous luxury, as did his courtiers. The same was true of England, where fingers were perfectly respectable eating implements even in the reign of Queen Anne.

Just as fellow guests at a dinner shared the serving dishes, so they shared the wine cup. There was an etiquette of drinking, just as there was of eating,

39] The vintage, early fifteenth century

but although the courtesy books in general condemned drunkenness, the rules they laid down must have tended to encourage it. It was regarded as good manners to drink only three times during the course of a meal. Those who followed this precept must have felt compelled to stoke up generously on each occasion. At certain periods, it was considered bad manners to pass over to one's neighbour a half-full (or half-empty) cup. The guest, therefore, had to drain his cup—hastily, perhaps, if his neighbour wore a thirsty look—before passing it over to be refilled. If one's neighbour offered a full cup, it was regarded as bad manners not to accept it and drink deeply from it. By the Renaissance, too, the old custom of exchanging toasts had been revived, though not, according to Giovanni della Casa, in Italy where 'thank God, among the many pests which have come to us from beyond the mountains, this vilest one has not yet reached us, of regarding drunkenness as not merely a laughing matter, but even a merit'.

Italians might not approve of drunkenness, but they did like their wine strong. The favourites in Della Casa's time were *greco*, made from a grape which had originally been imported from Crete, and *malvasia* or Malmsey, from Greece by way of Crete. The local favourite in northern Italy was the highly alcoholic *vernaccia*, white, sweet and rough. There was also a red *vernaccia* which was exported and known in England as vernage.

France, however, then as now was the wine-producing country *par excellence*. From the ninth to the thirteenth centuries, the most popular wines were those from Mâcon, Cahors, Rheims, Choisy, Montargis, Marne, Meulan and Orléanais. The modern visitor to France finds it slightly eerie to see road signs pointing to Vouvray, Pouilly or Montbazillac; the effect is much the same when one finds the names of Beaune, Saint Emilion, Chablis and Epernay casually mentioned in thirteenth-century literature. Champagne, by about 1400, was becoming the favourite drink of kings and queens—though not, it should be added, the sparkling wine of today. The fizz did not appear until the seventeenth century. But in spite of the richness of their own wines, the French imported others from the Rhine, Cyprus and Spain.

By the early thirteenth century, Bordeaux wines (or wines of Gascony, as they were called) were being shipped to the Hansa towns, Flanders and England—where they were known as clairet and drunk only weeks old. A hundred years later, the English were also enjoying Spanish and Portuguese wines, and, like most other Europeans, Malmsey. By the end of the fifteenth century much of Europe's Malmsey was coming from Madeira. In 1418 Henry the Navigator had sent one of his captains to appropriate the island, which was covered by almost impenetrable forest. Captain Zarco cleared the forest by the simple expedient of lighting a fire which, it is said, raged for seven years. Wood ash and the leaf mould of centuries helped to turn the soil into the most fertile in the world, and the Portuguese planted sugar and the Malmsey vine. It was a profitable operation for everybody (except the Turks, who had occupied Greece, the original home of the wine). Europe had its Malmsey at 1s 4d the gallon, and sugar, which had hitherto come by the spice routes from India and cost up to 2s per lb, dropped to between 10d and 4d per lb.

Much wine was drunk young and was probably very acid. But mediaeval householders had their own ways of improving it; some of them must presumably have been efficacious, although they scarcely sound so. Bad wine was said to be improved by subjection to frost; tart wine could be sweetened by the addition of a basketful of ripe black grapes; boiled egg whites and shells were to be fried and then suspended (in a bag) in the cask, to clear muddy wine; and a basket of sand, well washed in Seine water, would remedy bitterness. (Since half the sewage of Paris drained into the Seine, it might have been preferable to leave the sand unwashed.)

Ordinary wine was drunk during meals, but after the cloths had been removed wafers and hippocras were served. Hippocras, about which poets waxed lyrical, was one of the spiced wines known as 'piments' which were customarily drunk as liqueurs. A late fourteenth-century recipe favoured by the Goodman of Paris gives some idea of its impact:

'Take a quarter of very fine cinnamon selected by tasting it, and half a quarter of fine flour of cinnamon, an ounce of selected string ginger, fine and white, and an ounce of grain [cardamom], a sixth of nutmegs and galingale together, and pound them all together. And when you would make your hippocras, take a good half ounce of this powder and two quarters of sugar and mix them with a quart of wine by Paris measure.'

Hippocras was still being drunk in the eighteenth century although it had become rather less pungent.

'Take a quart of good white wine, a pound of sugar, an ounce of cinnamon bark, a little mace, two whole white peppercorns, a lemon cut in quarters. Leave to infuse for some time; then pass your hippocras through the strainer three or four times. You can give it the scent of musk and amber by putting a bead of it, ground with sugar and wrapped in cotton, in the point of the strainer.'

The name, hippocras, was derived from the type of strainer used, which was known as Hippocrates' Sleeve.

Faithful—to the last gasp—to his spices, the mediaeval diner finished his hippocras and wafers, moved to another room, and sat down to Malmsey or

some other sweet wine—and spices. This time, they were taken neat, sometimes in powder form, as an aid to digestion; ginger, cardamom, coriander
and cinnamon bark were among them. Sometimes, on grand occasions, spices
would be supplemented by comfits and preserves, all of them piled into
fanciful representations of lions, swans or deer, and embossed with any royal
or noble arms which seemed appropriate to the occasion.

In France wine was every man's drink. Taverners, who appeared in the
twelfth century, sold wine in small quantities, but for a cask of good wine the
householder went to the port de la Grève and chose his wine on the very ship
which had brought it to Paris. On one side there were the ships from
Burgundy, on the other those from the Ile de France and Brie. Official
gaugers were present to check the contents of each cask. There were a few
breweries in Paris in the twelfth century, but these gradually disappeared.
They returned in 1428 when wine was dear. Afterwards, ale became almost
popular, but its wide distribution was always hampered by the fact that
production was banned in times of grain shortage.

40] A fifteenth-century Paris
wine-gauger at work

In England vineyards were mainly attached to monastic foundations and began to disappear when Henry VIII dissolved the monasteries. Not that they had ever been over-fruitful, for they had been cultivated according to Palladius, i.e. in a style more suited to the Mediterranean. Much more common drinks in England were ale, cider, mead and metheglin which were brewed on the manor in early days, and in almost every household after the collapse of the manorial system. Mead, a drink of great antiquity, was made of honey and spring water, boiled together and then fermented, while metheglin was a honey liquor flavoured with herbs. In spite of the prevalence of home brewing, there was still a place for commercial brewers, although their products had to be passed by an ale-conner before they were sold.

Early in the fifteenth century hops were introduced from Flanders, but the technique of adding bitter herbs to perfectly good ale was regarded with some suspicion. The resulting brew was little valued; when Henry V was engaged on the siege of Rouen in 1418 beer was supplied from London for his troops at less than half the price of ale. And in 1424 brewers who added hops to their ale were charged with adulterating it. A century later, Henry VIII tried to ban the use of hops, but by then it was too late. The bitter herbs had a preservative effect, and the English had begun to realize that beer kept better than ale. They had also begun to acquire a taste for it. By the end of the sixteenth century, beer and sherry-sack were universal favourites.

While the English housewife brewed her own beer, the Scots wife was purposefully engaged in distilling her own whisky, which was a familiar drink in the Highlands by the fifteenth century. Even fine ladies were expected to be adept at this domestic task. The process of distilling alcohol had been discovered by the Arabs in the early Middle Ages, and a treatise on wine and spirits by the famous thirteenth-century Salerno teacher, Arnaldus de Villa Nuova, became almost the standard work on the subject. To Arnaldus, distilled alcohol was the 'water of life', and the name persisted— *aqua vitae*, *eau de vie* and *uisge beatha*, the Gaelic term which was later corrupted into 'whisky'.

The sixteenth-century European—like his ancestors and his heirs—downed his drink in large quantities. Then, as always, well-meaning experts had their own remedies to offer. Whereas the ancient Egyptians had favoured cabbage as a specific against drunkenness, the Elizabethan Sir Hugh Platt suggested: 'Drink first a good large draught of salad oil, for that will float upon the wine which you shall drink, and suppress the spirits from ascending into the brain. Also what quantity soever of new milk you drink first, you may well drink thrice as much wine after, without danger of being drunk. But', he added cautiously, 'how sick you shall be with this prevention, I will not here determine.'

Six

Columbus set out in 1492 in search of spices for the rich. Instead, he discovered a continent which was to provide two great staple foods for the European poor—maize and potatoes. When the Admiral of the Ocean Sea landed in Cuba with his men, the American Indians 'gave them some cooked roots that had the flavour of chestnuts [sweet potatoes, or yams]. . . . They also saw much land planted to the roots mentioned above, to kidney beans, to some kind of horse beans, and to a grain resembling panic grass that they call maize and is most tasty, boiled, roasted, or ground into flour.' For men accustomed to the arid lands of Spain, the Caribbean islands were unimaginably fertile. When Columbus returned to Haiti after a brief expedition, he found that 'the melons were ripe enough to eat, though they had been planted less than two months before; cucumbers had come up in twenty days, and a native wild grape-vine had already produced large fine grapes while they were still cultivating it. Next day, March 30, a labourer harvested spikes of wheat which had been planted [with seed brought from Spain] at the end of January; they also picked chickpeas larger than those they had planted. All the seeds they had sown sprouted in three days and were ready to eat by the twenty-fifth day. Fruit stones planted in the ground sprouted in seven days. . . . Sugar canes [also from Spain] germinated in seven days.'

Four times in all Columbus sailed to the Caribbean. On the last voyage he was accompanied by his son, Ferdinand. The first voyage had taken a little over two months, but the fourth was a very different matter. Food ran short, and even fish were so scarce that the sailors were reduced to subsisting on shark. 'Some viewed it as an evil omen and others thought it poor fishing,' wrote Ferdinand, 'but all did shark the honour of eating it; for by that time we had been over eight months at sea and had consumed all the meat and fish that we had brought from Spain. And what with the heat and the dampness, even the biscuit was so full of worms that, God help me, I saw many wait until nightfall to eat the porridge made of it, so as not to see the worms.'

Columbus died discredited. Instead of spices, he had brought back the bad news that a large land mass would have to be circumnavigated before any westward route to the Indies could be opened. Nevertheless, in the decade that followed his death, Spanish adventurers set out from Europe to join the settlers he had left behind in the Caribbean. Cortes lived in Cuba for some years before he embarked on his conquest of the Aztecs of Mexico. Pizarro had settled in Panama before tales of fabulous riches sent him off in search of Peru and the gold of the Incas.

When Cortes and his four hundred followers first looked down into the valley in which the Aztec capital, Tenochtitlan, lay, they were dazzled by the white buildings and lush green gardens, set in blue waters and ringed by massive hills. 'Gazing on such wonderful sights, we did not know what to say or whether what appeared before us was real', wrote Bernal Diaz del Castillo. 'On one side in the land there were great cities and in the lake ever so many more, and the lake itself was crowded with canoes, and in the cause-way were many bridges at intervals, and in front of us stood the great city.' It was very different from the rusty hues of Spain, and from the new encampments of the Caribbean, and Cortes was to destroy it.

But the first time the conquistadors came, they came in peace. 'Montezuma took Cortes by the hand and told him to look at his great city and all the other cities that were standing in the water and the many other towns and the land around the lake . . . and it was a wonderful thing to behold.' In the market place, recorded Bernal Diaz, 'we were astonished at the number of people and the quantity of merchandise that it contained, and at the good order and control that was maintained. . . . Each kind of merchandise was kept by itself and had its fixed place marked out. . . . Let us go on and speak of those who sold beans and sage and other vegetables and herbs . . . and to those who sold fowls, cocks with wattles, rabbits, hare, deer, mallards, young dogs [specially bred for food] and other things of that sort in their part of the market, and let us also mention the fruiterers and the women who sold cooked food, dough and tripe in their part of the market; then every sort of pottery made in a thousand different forms from great water jars to little jugs, these also had a place to themselves; then those who sold honey and honey paste, and other dainties like nut paste. . . . I am forgetting those who sell salt, and those who make stone knives, and how they split them off the stone itself.'

With one or two exceptions, the market of Tenochtitlan does not sound very different from the markets of London, Paris or Venice. Certainly, it was quieter and more rigidly controlled. It was probably cleaner, too, for the Aztecs had few domesticated animals and no need of the great meat slaughter-houses which polluted the streets and rivers of European cities. The Mexican diet was mainly vegetarian. What we know as the 'turkey' provided the main source of meat, and this was supplemented by fish and at the time of the great

42] A German view
of the turkey,
late sixteenth century

41] A Mexican artist's view of the turkey, mid-sixteenth century

seasonal bird migrations by ducks, geese and other wild fowl, by an occasional trapped rabbit, and by the special, hairless breed of dog—a larger ancestor of the modern Chihuahua—which the Mexican Indians raised for food.

The turkey was imported into Europe at a very early stage indeed. The conquest of Mexico was begun in 1519, and the turkey was known in Europe by 1523. But the bird's name echoes a long history of confusion. What seems to have happened is this. The bird was brought to Europe by the Spaniards. Spain was on the English sea route to the Levant, and it was not long before the Levant merchants—'Turkey merchants', as they were called—discovered the bird and took it to England. Not knowing its real name (or perhaps merely reluctant to make the effort of pronouncing it), the English called it simply the Turkey-bird. Many historians find this explanation difficult to accept because, in the sixteenth century, the turkey was sometimes confused with the guinea fowl, which was introduced into Britain in about 1530 and called the 'Turkie henne'. Since the guinea fowl, however, was brought by the Portuguese from Guinea on the coast of West Africa, the Turkish attribution makes no sense at all unless it is assumed that the turkey reached Britain first, followed by the guinea fowl which, being smaller, was then assumed to be the hen bird of the species.

Confusion over the turkey was not confined to Britain. In France it was called the *coq d'Inde* (or Indian cock), a name which was finally corrupted into the modern *dinde* or *dindon*. At first sight, the name seems to be explained by the fact that the new Spanish territories in America were still referred to as the Spanish Indies. The same might be said in the case of the German name, *indianische Henn*. Unfortunately, the Germans also called it the *Calecutische Hahn*, while the Dutch named it *Kalkoen*. Both of these names imply that the bird originated in Calicut, in south India. It is possible that it had, in fact, reached India early enough to be brought to continental Europe by the Portuguese during the normal course of their trading with the East. From Latin America via the Philippines—a Spanish possession governed, not from Spain but from Mexico—to India would have been a simple enough journey. Certainly, by the beginning of the seventeenth century, the Mughal emperor possessed three turkey cocks. But although the Indian name for the turkey comes geographically closer to accuracy than any other, it is still some hundreds of miles off the mark. The Indians called the bird *peru*—and in Peru, unlike Mexico, the turkey was unknown at the time of the Spanish conquest. Whatever the truth of the turkey's wanderings, it was well established in Europe by the end of the sixteenth century. Indeed, a German cookery book was able to suggest twenty different ways of serving it.

Just as cowrie shells were used for currency in India and, to some extent, in China, the people of Mexico and central America treated cacao beans as money. European kings levied taxes partly in cash and partly in casks of wine or creels of fish. Montezuma demanded bags of cacao, jars of honey, bins of maize and kidney beans, bales of sage and purslane. European kings, from Charlemagne onwards, had many mouths to feed. So, too, did Montezuma. Three hundred guests and a thousand guards and attendants were not unusual. Montezuma, however, seems to have been rather less inclined to hold open house than his predecessors. When, in about 1430, the majordomo of Tetzcuco had been obliged to supply the palace and court for seventy days, he had to send each day just under a hundred bushels of maize, four bags of cacao beans (not as money, but to make chocolate and other drinks), one hundred birds, twenty loaves of salt, twenty baskets of large and twenty of small chilli peppers, ten baskets of tomatoes, and four hundred thousand tortillas.

The tortilla, a maize cake, was the staple food of Mexico, Central America

43] A young Mexican girl being taught by her
mother how to make tortillas

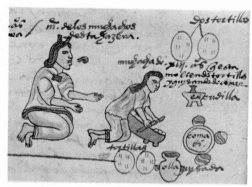

and the western strip of South America between the Andes and the Pacific. Maize became known in Europe by its Cuban name, because it was in Cuba that the conquistadors first became acquainted with the new type of corn. In Mexico it was known as *tlaolli*. There, the grains were boiled in water with the addition of wood charcoal or a little lime to loosen the skin, which was then removed by rubbing between the hands. The moist grain was next crushed on a concave stone with water and lime juice to form a paste, and this paste was kneaded into cakes ten inches across and just over half an inch thick; these were cooked on an earthenware griddle which rested on the hearth. In Peru, the technique was somewhat different. There, the ears of corn were used dry rather than moist and were ground into a flour which could be used for *polenta*-like dishes as well as for tortillas.

Most Mexicans in Aztec times lived on tortillas and boiled kidney beans, although on ceremonial occasions there would be toasted maize and turkey stew, or perhaps *guacamole*, a thick mixture of tomato, avocado pear and chilli pepper, served with an insect which was a delicacy in Aztec times (as it is today), the slug of the maguey plant.

On other ceremonial occasions, turkey stew was replaced by *tlacatlaolli*— maize-and-man stew. Cannibalism was an accepted part of Aztec ritual. The human heart was the finest offering man could make to the gods, and the Aztecs went to war to capture prisoners whose living hearts could be sacrificed. It was believed that, as the gods drew power from the human heart, so man could increase his own strength by consuming the strength, i.e. the body, of one who had proved a worthy adversary. Such reasoning was by no means unique to the Aztecs; there are implications of it in the earliest history of many peoples. But to the sixteenth century, the discovery of such practices in what was then 'the modern world' seemed barbaric in the extreme. The conquistadors were horrified at the sight of the skull racks of Tenochtitlan, relics of apparently numberless blood-sacrifices to the sun and subsequent cannibal banquets. After the priests had torn the heart from the victim, the skull was hung on the skull rack, one thigh was presented to the supreme council and other choice cuts to various nobles. The remainder of the body was returned to the victim's original captor who took it home and had it cooked with maize into a man stew, which was then reverently consumed by all the family.

Man stew was not destined to enter the dietary of Europe in company with the turkey, the tomato and maize. Nor was the favourite drink of Mexico— *pulque*, the 'white wine of the earth'—which is made from the yucca-like maguey plant. Ten years after planting, the maguey sends up a flower stalk

44] Mexican Indians cultivating a walled garden. The plant with two flower spikes, left centre, is probably intended to represent the *pulque* maguey

as tall as a tree. This is cut to the base while in full flower, and sap oozes up into the hollow of the plant. Each plant yields up to fifteen pints of sap every day until it withers. The liquid is carefully collected and fermented to make a kind of beer. In Aztec times *pulque* was not only a welcome reviver for the hardworking peasant but a useful source of nutrition, for the Mexican diet was by no means rich in green vegetables. The maguey plant was, in many ways, as valuable to Mexico as the bamboo was to China. It provided an excellent drink; its fibres could be twisted into rope and woven into baskets, or even into heavy clothing; its thorns provided sharp, strong needles; and the leaves were useful for thatching huts.

In the Peru of the Incas, the conquistadors found a civilization as regimented as that of the Aztecs but much less bloodthirsty. There appears to have been little or no cannibalism, and human sacrifice was reserved for only the most awesome occasions. Climatically, too, Peru was very different from Mexico, and the diet of the population varied in relation to altitude and temperature. In the cold highlands of the Andes, the Spaniards found a strange new vegetable, the potato, replacing maize—which did not grow at altitudes higher than 11,000 feet—as a staple food. The Andean peoples preserved their potatoes by allowing them to freeze and then thaw, after which the moisture was squeezed out and they were allowed to dry.

By 1573 the potato was under cultivation in Spain, and by 1588 it was known in the Low Countries, then under Spanish rule. A German cookery book was already offering potato recipes, and in 1598 the first cookery book published by a woman appeared in Switzerland; it included a recipe for a potato dish which is still loved by the Swiss today, *Kartoffelnrösti*. Italy at first made slight use of the new vegetable, as did England. But although the specimens which Drake brought back from Virginia in 1584 seem to have made few early converts in southern England, they did stimulate cultivation in Ireland, where the potato soon became a universal food. And there, for the time being, distribution of the potato ended. France, for almost two hundred years, would have nothing at all to do with what Diderot was to describe as 'an Egyptian fruit whose cultivation may possibly have some value in the colonies'.

The potato, the turkey, the tomato, maize, avocado pears, Lima beans, scarlet runners, string beans, chocolate, peanuts, vanilla, red peppers and green peppers, tapioca (from the manioc plant)—all these Central and South American products have become so commonplace in Europe that few people realize where they originated.

Fortunately for the Pilgrim Fathers, maize and the turkey were also to be found on the coast of North America. Maize was unfamiliar to them because, although it had been brought to Europe many decades earlier, it had become popular only around the Mediterranean coasts, but they were delighted to recognize the turkey. True to tradition, there was some slight confusion over the name, but this time it was very slight. The settlers' turkey was the North American Indians' *furkee*. With it the pilgrims were able to give thanks for their first harvest in 1621. 'Our harvest being gotten in', wrote Edward Winslow, 'our governor sent four men on fowling, that so we might, after a special manner, rejoice together after we had gathered the fruit of our labours. They four in one day killed as much fowl as, with a little help beside, served the company almost a week.'

Without maize and the help of friendly Indians, few of the early settlers in North America would have survived. They had armed themselves, not with cattle, food, agricultural tools, clothes, malt, fish hooks, nails or medicaments, but with cannon, armour, a few gardening implements, and onion, bean and pea seeds. They themselves were not practical labourers or craftsmen, carpenters or blacksmiths. The land was rich in game, the waters alive with fish, the woods full of edible berries, but—particularly in Virginia, the earliest settlement (1607)—the settlers seemed incapable of making use of

45] As early as 1563, maize was known round the coasts of the Mediterranean, though not in northern Europe. Arcimboldo incorporated it with oats, wheat and a variety of fruits in his representation of 'Summer'

them. They did not know how to trap game, and rarely managed to shoot any. They had no fishing tackle. Death seemed so near that fear of it prevented them from trying to eat unfamiliar berries, in case they might be poisonous.

In Virginia, Captain John Smith—the third and most dynamic leader of the colonists—traded with the Indians and acquired sixteen bushels of life-giving corn. The Indians of Virginia made maize cakes on much the same principle as the people of Mexico, first boiling the grains and pounding them to a paste. William Strachey described the method in 1612. The Indians, he said, 'receive the flour in a platter of wood, which, blending with water, they make into flat, broad cakes [which] they call *apones*, which covering with ashes till they be baked . . . and then washing them in fair water, [they] let dry with their own heat'. The settlers took over the technique, and the name. The Indian *apone* became the American corn pone, the first 'bread' the settlers knew in their adopted land.

In New England, too, the settlers learned from Indians how to grow and use maize. They were also taught how to hold a clambake, which has since become a national institution. The method is particularly interesting, because it reflects a cooking technique used in prehistoric times, before cooking-pots were invented. A fire was built on large stones and brushed away when the stones were white-hot. A layer of seaweed was laid on the stones, then a layer of clams, another layer of seaweed, then ears of corn protected by extra corn husks, a further layer of seaweed and finally, perhaps, fish wrapped in leaves. The whole was covered with a large blanket of wet cloth, canvas or animal hide, which was kept moist throughout the cooking time (about forty-five minutes). The blanket was firmly anchored around the edges so that none of the salty steam should escape.

Hominy, succotash, Boston baked beans—all seem to have originated with the American Indian. The English settlers who took Master Gervase Markham's invaluable cookery book, *The English House-wife*, with them to the new land must have found it of scant use. Not that they threw it away; many copies must have been treasured against the day when it was possible for the immigrants to achieve a sophisticated cuisine. Curiously enough, Gervase Markham's recipe for a salad in 1615 is much closer to the modern American salad than to an English one:

'Take a good quantity of blanched almonds, and with your shredding knife cut them grossly; then take as many raisins of the sun, clean washed and the stones picked out, as many figs shred like the almonds, as many capers, twice so many olives, and as many currants as of all the rest, clean washed, a good handful of the small tender leaves of red sage and spinach. Mix all these well together with good store of sugar, and lay them in the bottom of a great dish, then put unto them vinegar and oil, and scrape more sugar over all. Then take oranges and lemons, and paring away the outward shells, cut them into thin slices. Then with those slices cover the salad all over; which done, take the fine leaf of the red cabbage and with them cover the oranges and lemons all over. Then over those red leaves lay another course of old olives, and the slices of well-pickled cucumbers, together with the very inward heart of cabbage-lettuce cut into slices; then adorn the sides of the dish and the top of the salad with more slices of lemons and oranges, and so serve it up.'

In the meantime, however, the settlers made do with hominy, which was
a porridge, pudding or bread made from coarse corn meal; succotash, a purée
of beans mixed with whole, boiled corn kernels and anything else that
happened to be handy; and Boston baked beans, the slow-cooked dish of
beans and molasses that helped the Puritan housewife devote the Sabbath to
prayer instead of food preparation. The beans and molasses combination was
typically Indian, for the American Indian seasoned his food with maple sugar
rather than the much less accessible salt. This may, indeed, go part of the way
towards explaining the traditional American fondness for sweet and sweet-
cooked foods.

One cooking technique practised by the founding fathers appears to have
come, not from local Indians but from Mexico. This was barbecuing. In
Mexico the Spaniards had seen fish being smoke-dried on lattices of green
wood and had adapted the idea for roasting large joints of meat. They called
the roasting frame *barbacoa*, which became 'barbecue' as the technique drifted
northwards from the Spanish territories. It may be mentioned here that the

46] An early barbecue. Brazil, *c*. 1564

buccaneers of the Spanish Main are said to have derived their name from their habit of barbecuing food; the word buccaneer comes from the French *boucaner*, which means to smoke-dry.

As new settlers arrived in America from various European countries, they brought their favourite dishes with them, some to become naturalized, some to be adapted for new ingredients. The English brought apple pie. The French introduced chowder (from *chaudière*, a fish-kettle). The Dutch took cookies (*koekjes*), coleslaw (*kool*: cabbage, and *sla*: salad) and waffles—although a modern writer, Louis P. DeGouy, claims that waffles were not Dutch in origin. On the contrary, he says, they were invented quite unintentionally in England in 1204, when Sir Giles Whimple inadvertently sat upon an oatcake while dressed in a suit of chain mail.

It was easier for immigrants in America to adapt themselves to new foods than it was for them to accept being deprived of their favourite drinks. In New England, attempts were made to grow barley and hops, but these did

47] Before the American War of Independence, punch had become such an institution that the punchbowl was used to lend a homely touch to a ceremonial portrait

not flourish. Fruit trees, on the other hand, did very well indeed, and cider soon became the everyday drink. Apple trees also produced the liquor known as applejack; the more refined version of this was apple brandy; the rougher version, which involved freezing as well as fermenting, was highly potent— almost pure alcohol. Some people called it 'essence of lockjaw'. Once the colonists had begun to settle down, they discovered a taste for the rum which could be (and was) imported in great quantities from the West Indies. Just before the American War of Independence, it was estimated that the colonists were downing three imperial gallons of rum per head, per year. Whisky, too, followed rapidly in the footsteps of Scots and Irish settlers, who reached America in appreciable numbers early in the eighteenth century. Dutch and German settlers in Pennsylvania had discovered that the land was suitable for barley and hops and had begun brewing beer there; barley was also the basis for whisky. Towards the end of the eighteenth century, however, the people of Kentucky discovered that it was possible to make whisky from maize, and Bourbon whiskey was born in Bourbon County, Kentucky. (In Scotland,

48] Rich land and even richer livestock on the Cornell Farm in Bucks County, Pennsylvania, 1848

England and Canada, the word is spelled whisky; in Ireland and the United States, it is whiskey.) When George Washington's government tried to raise money by imposing an excise tax on whiskey, it found itself faced in Pennsylvania with the 'Whiskey Rebellion', and had to send in the militia. The Pennsylvania farmer/distillers afterwards decided that redskin warriors were better than paleface excisemen and moved off westwards.

It was the British attempt to tax America's tea which precipitated the American War of Independence, but some historians argue—rather more convincingly—that the rot set in much earlier, with the Molasses Act of 1733, which was designed to make the colonists give up West Indian rum in favour of the British product.

Certainly, alcohol was one of the mainstays of eighteenth-century America. It helped to keep out the cold. It quenched the majestic thirst that resulted from too much salt meat and fish. It was a social ice-breaker. And it even became a political tradition. When George Washington ran for the legislature in 1758, his agent doled out almost one and a half quarts of rum, beer, wine and cider to every voter. Washington himself was slightly worried about dispensing such hospitality to the electorate—but only in case his agent had been too niggardly! It was, perhaps, hardly surprising that a strong temperance movement should have emerged in the nineteenth century. At its spearhead were respectable ladies who carried the movement into the home with such cookery books as the *Temperance Housekeeper's Almanac* and *Christianity in the Kitchen*. Mrs Horace Mann, author of the latter work, stated categorically (if somewhat obscurely) that 'there is no more prolific cause of bad morals than abuses of diet', and denounced not only alcohol, but pork, wedding cake and turtle soup as un-Christian.

Once America became independent, expansion and enterprise were not only necessary but purposeful. The nation had, so to speak, become self-employed; it was working for its own profit, not for the profit of a distant and unsympathetic monarchy. Slowly, the population began to overflow into hitherto unknown territory, into the vast lands in the heart of the continent, and then farther and farther west. The people of the eastern seaboard had settled down into a pattern of existence not too far removed from that of their contemporaries in Europe. The city housewife had her servants, her table silver, her coffee, white bread, imported cheeses, salads and white loaf sugar. She had her European cookery books, too, and after 1796 was even able to buy a real American cookery book, written by 'An American Orphan' (Amelia Simmons) and published in Connecticut. The housewife on a prosperous farm lived almost as comfortably as her city sister, though her daily tasks were more extensive. Such a woman as Mrs James C. Cornell, for example, whose husband's farm stock starred at the Agricultural Society shows in Pennsylvania, probably supervised the running of her household, the dairying, the pickle-making and the preserving, and also had to ensure that the smoke-house was hung with meat and game for the winter, and that the root cellar had its appointed store of barrels of apples, bins of potatoes; its quota of dried corn, beans, pumpkins and squash.

The poorer farm wife lived closer to American beginnings. She sweetened her pies with maple sugar or molasses, made puddings from maize (or Indian corn, as she called it), cooked fresh meat or fish only when her man had a good day's hunting. If the soil was not friendly, the poor American farmer upped sticks and moved on in search of better; indeed, it was the poor farmer, not the rich, who colonized the continent. In 1900 a Tennessee pastor argued that, without Indian corn, these farmers and the other adventurers who travelled westwards across America would have taken a hundred years longer to reach the Rockies. If they had relied on wheat for their food grain, they would have had to halt for a year to cultivate it every time they ran short. But even a woman could grow corn in a patch around the cabin, with no need to plough or hoe. In six weeks from planting, the ears were fit to roast, and afterwards it could be dried for flour. Nor did it, like wheat, need to be harvested all at once. When the settlers moved on again, they took with them a few sacks of dried, or 'parched' corn, and supplies of what we would today call convenience foods. If it were winter, the housewife would make a bean porridge and freeze it with a string through it by which it might be hung up out of the way. When it was needed a piece could be broken off, melted and eaten. There were also johnnycakes, cornmeal pancakes which could be kept (though not very appetizingly) for long periods. The name johnnycake was derived either from the Indian 'shawnee' cake, or from 'journey cake', because supplies were universally carried on long journeys. Many travellers also took 'pocket soup' with them, the ancestor of the modern bouillon cube. Basically, it was an aspic made from heavily concentrated veal stock or from a cheaper stock made from meat and pigs' trotters. The aspic was cut into pieces, and when the traveller needed a bowl of soup he simply dissolved a piece in hot water.

More, perhaps, than in any other country, the American cuisine is a mirror of history—of mixed races, of friendly Indians (and of Indian wars), of territorial expansion, and of the natural riches of a vast continent. Look, for example, through the index of an American cookery book. There are Baked Alaska (originally known as Alaska-Florida), Ambushed Asparagus, Blueberry Pie, Shaker Loaf, Burgoo, Maryland Chicken, Snickerdoodles, Spoon Bread, Cowpoke Beans, Mint Julep, Planked Shad, Hush Puppies, Jambalaya, Pandowdy, Pecan Pie, Philadelphia Pepper Pot, Moravian Sugar Cake, Naples Biscuits, Swedish Meatballs, Indian Pudding, Haymaker's Switchel, Whaler's Toddy . . .

Seven

By 1650, Europe's centuries of adventure were coming to an end. Most of the world as we know it today had been charted. It was spices which had set the age of discovery in motion, but ironically enough, as discovery gave way to trade and then to empire, Europe grew tired of spices. By 1700, they were cheaper, more easily available—and much less used in European cooking.

The new lands, however, gave new foods to Europe as well as greater supplies of fruits which, though long known, had always been prohibitively expensive. The Dutch East India Company brought back seeds and plants from the territories it had acquired in the east, and cultivation began under the most favourable conditions that could be contrived in northern climes. The fruits grown with such care were not, perhaps, very fine, but they must certainly have helped to break down the old resistance to fruit as a food and to encourage the import of more luscious varieties from the Mediterranean countries. Certainly, the markets of the north began to provide a feast for the eye as well as the stomach, inspiring Dutch and Flemish artists to marvels of still-life painting. In 1636, Jan Davidsz de Heem even moved his dwelling to Antwerp, because 'there one could have rare fruits of all kinds, large plums, peaches, cherries, oranges, lemons, grapes and others, in finer condition and state of ripeness to draw from life'.

In England, too, rare fruits were beginning to be cultivated. At Whitechapel, one nursery gardener specialized in nectarines and peaches, dwarf plums and cherries. Mulberries and figs grew surprisingly well in London's soil, and strawberries flourished. Vegetable gardens grew steadily in number, their produce coming up lush and leafy as a result of rich manures. Horse manure was, of course, plentiful, but farmers and market gardeners supplemented it with the harvest of the scavengers' rakes—that mixture of human manure and household refuse which was daily gathered up and carted off from the streets of London. It probably did the vegetables no harm, although the

49] To De Heem in the seventeenth century, a 'still life' of food meant overflowing riches

50] Ex-Queen Christina of Sweden dines with the Pope, at tables banked with sugar sculptures

practice offered excellent ammunition for anyone who felt inclined to complain about either the quality or price of the produce on sale at Covent Garden and Spitalfields. At the beginning of the eighteenth century, the Society of Gardeners was formed, and by the end of the century—when the British were at long last beginning to accept other vegetables than cabbage and onions as a regular item of diet—there were two hundred and fifty market gardens in the district of Ealing alone. Fresh fruit became fashionable rather more quickly than vegetables, once the barriers had been broken, but many middle-class households clung to the dried fruits they had used for so long in such a multitude of dishes. Dates, figs, and 'raisins of the sun' maintained their popularity, and Zante currants were enjoying such a vogue in 1632 that William Lithgow remarked: 'Some liquorous lips, forsooth, can now hardly digest bread, pasties, broth and bag-puddings without these currants!'

Fruit had an established place on French and Italian menus by the middle of the seventeenth century, although in Italy it had to compete with sweetmeats and those masterpieces of sugar sculpture known as *trionfi*. When Queen Christina of Sweden dined with the Pope in 1668, both appear to have been virtually hidden from view behind the sugar table-decorations.

It was not unusual for the great to dine in public, in the manner shown in Sevin's drawing, watched by guests invited to observe the spectacle. The ladies, it will be noted, were expected to view from behind the arras. Such dinners were something of a trial, even for monarchs accustomed to the gaze of the curious, and protocol made Queen Christina's dinner with the Pope more trying than most. She could not be permitted to sit at the same table as His Holiness, but had to be content with a lower one. She was no longer a ruling princess, so her tablecloth was merely of silk while the Pope's was of velvet. The two diners were seated so far apart that it was impossible for them to converse directly, and any exchange of civilities had to be made through the good offices of one Monsignore Febei, who stood between them. Conversation would, perhaps, have been difficult in any case, since the banquet was accompanied not only by choral music but by a sermon preached by a Jesuit father. After four meat dishes, a large number of desserts, fruit, sweetmeats and confectionery, the cloths were removed and, the meal being over, the queen was permitted to seat herself at the Pope's table. Not for long. The Pope had had enough, and since protocol required that he should be the one to leave the banqueting hall first, he did so after the briefest conversation that civility would allow.

Dining at the court of Louis XIV, if slightly less strained, was no less formal. Kings still expected to be poisoned by design rather than by inferior cooking, and by the time the ritual procession of guards, waiters and officials had made its stately way from the kitchens to the royal chamber, the king's food was already well on the way to being cool. By the time His Majesty had been summoned to table and a gentleman-in-waiting had tasted the first dish for poison, it was wholly cold. Louis XIV was a powerful ruler and an ingenious one. If he had really cared about food, it should not have been beyond his capacity to devise some method of ensuring that his dinner was hot as well as harmless.

Gastronomically speaking, the reign of Louis XIV was notable for something more important than the grandeur of its banquets. It saw the publication of three cookery books by François Pierre de La Varenne which marked the development of a new style of cooking. The French had been slow to produce cookery books—the only printed work to appear before La Varenne's day had been the fourteenth-century *Le Viandier*, by Taillevent, which appeared about 1490, shortly after printing was introduced into France. It is probable, therefore, that the style of cooking described in La Varenne's works had been developing for some time.

The most striking feature of the new cuisine was its lack of spices. La Varenne frowned on them. He disapproved, too, of the porridge-stews of meat and almonds which had dominated French cooking for so long. He accepted vegetables as existing in their own right, rather than as ingredients for soup and trimmings for meat. Fifty years later, under the influence of La Varenne, a Frenchman could for the first time afford to be supercilious about the English attitude to vegetables: 'Another time they will have a piece of boiled beef, and then they salt it some days beforehand, and besiege it with five or six heaps of cabbage, carrots, turnips or some other herbs or roots, well peppered and salted, and swimming in butter.' The French were more refined. La Varenne made much use of globe artichokes, introduced the stuffed mushroom to France, rendered the truffle—which had been treated as a pickle and then justly forgotten until Marie de Medici's cooks reintroduced it—respectable, and devised simple sauces based on the drippings of roast meat combined merely with vinegar, lemon juice, or verjuice (the juice of sorrel, sour grapes, green wheat, or crab apples). He gave serious consideration, too, to the humble egg, providing sixty different recipes in *Le Pastissier François*. This work—which first appeared in 1653, and whose 1655 reprint by the house of Elzevier became known as the most expensive cookery book in the world because it was so much sought after—also introduced puff pastry

51] Vinegar had always been widely used in French cooking, but La Varenne's new sauces must have given a fillip to the trade of the vinegar merchants (who also made mustard). Unfortunately, few sellers of vinegar can have been as appealing as Bonnard's fantasy figure

to the cookbook market. Puff pastry could not be made with oil, as earlier pastry had been, and butter soon became the preferred ingredient for all pastry. La Varenne also gave recipes for *pièces de four*, little cakes to be cooked in the little ovens which had 'lately come into use in some kitchens'. The ovens were known as *petits fours* and the name ultimately transferred itself to the miniature macaroons and other cakes we know as such today.

After half a century in the steel corset of the Sun King's court, it was hardly surprising that the French Régence should have unlaced itself with such evident joy. Stiffness was abandoned, morals relaxed, and even the nobility insisted on the luxury that Versailles had never known—hot food. The most elevated hosts began to dabble in cooking, and guests invaded the kitchens to 'help' the cooks. A new note began to be heard in cookery writing when Marin, in *Les Dons de Comus*, claimed that the bourgeoisie could eat like princes with 'proper pots and pans . . . fresh food purchased each morning and a good bouillon'. The acknowledgement that the bourgeoisie even existed was new

52] French pastry-makers might produce decorative marvels when
they turned their attention to pies, but that was one sphere in which
the English were acknowledged masters

to France, unlike England and Germany, where the 'ordinary housewife' had
been catered for since the end of the sixteenth century. Another French writer,
Menon, scorned 'third-class persons' in his *Nouveau Traité de la Cuisine*, published in 1739, the same year as Marin's book, but he mellowed as the years
passed and admitted not only third-class persons to his confidence but third-
class cuts of meat to his books.

In England, cookery books had been doing very nicely since the genre
proved itself profitable. Gervase Markham's *The English House-wife*, first published in 1615, was in its eighth edition by 1668, and *The Good Huswife* could
also purchase her *Jewell*, or *Treasurie*, or *Closet*, or *Handmaid*. These little books
were replete with activity. A housewife had to do more than supervise the
arrangement of a whole boar on a bed of parsley. She was expected to instruct
the servants, oversee the preserve-making, handle estate accounts, and mix
plague cures. In 1655, during the Commonwealth, the secrets of the Stuart
kitchens were revealed to a breathless (and presumably royalist) audience, in

The Queens Closet Opened. Henrietta Maria had apparently fed her late husband on such exotic dishes as Banbury tarts, quaking pudding and gooseberry fool. The unfortunate woman must have been very much in sympathy with her adopted country if the sales of the book are any criterion. It is more probable, however, that the title was a fiction of the author's imagination, a sales gimmick designed to boost circulation.

As French cooking became respected, English noblemen sent their cooks across the Channel to be trained. It was a fashion that did not last for very long—perhaps the French became altogether too superior to be tolerated. Certainly, by 1710 Patrick Lamb—a veteran among royal cooks—was firing the first shots in a battle that was to rage for the next two centuries at least. Britain's raw materials, he claimed (with limited justification), were unequalled anywhere else. Other countries sadly lacked Britain's 'substantial and wholesome plenty' and 'the quelque chose of France, and the vines of Italy' were no substitute for 'the surfeits and fevers they usually bring on such as deal in them'. Eliza Smith, one of the early women writers of cookery books, also scorned the 'quelque chose of France' (which, in England, became 'kickshaws') and was very acid on the subject of 'French messes' and upstart French chefs. So, too, was Hannah Glasse, though she did not hesitate to appropriate French recipes and fractured-French titles. By 1758, Sarah Phillips was beginning to foreshadow modern cooking techniques, particularly in the case of vegetables, where her injunctions to use minimum liquid and minimum cooking times shine like a good deed in a naughty world. She was a brisk lady—aggressively so, perhaps—and her instructions to 'hack it with a knife' or 'rip open the belly' are strongly reminiscent of mediaeval cookery manuscripts, which are full of such phrases as 'smite them in pieces' and 'hew them in gobbets'.

In 1727, Eliza Smith had rejected French cooking in favour of such delights as Cock Ale:

'Take ten gallons of ale, and a large cock, the older the better. Parboil the cock, flay him, and stamp him in a stone mortar till his bones are broken (you must craw and gut him when you flay him). Put the cock into two quarts of sack, and put to it three pounds of raisins of the sun stoned, some blades of mace, and a few cloves. Put all these into a canvas bag, and a little before you find the ale has done working, put the ale and bag together into a vessel. In a week or nine days' time bottle it up, fill the bottles but just above the necks, and leave the same to ripen as other ale.'

Towards the end of the nineteenth century, the British were turning up their noses at a similar preparation made by the 'primitive' Mongols of northern China. The mutton wine of the Mongols included among its ingredients one male sheep, two years old and castrated (very important, this), forty *catties* of cow's milk whisky, one pint of skim milk, soured and curdled, eight ounces of brown sugar, four ounces of honey, one *catty* of raisins, and an assortment of lesser items. The specific gravity of the product was apparently 0.98873 and the alcohol content was only 9.14 per cent! The Chinese, at least, had the grace to regard this as a medicinal product, to be taken only by the aged, and in small quantities. Eliza Smith, however, seems to have treated Cock Ale as a general-purpose drink.

Practical ladies in England continued to vie with the chefs of royal and noble households in producing cookery books, and it was the late Victorian era before the ladies finally gained the upper hand, in England, if not— definitely not—in France. French chefs, however, were just as capable of borrowing from the English cuisine as English housewives were from the French, and just as capable of mangling a foreign language. In the eighteenth century the word 'rostbif' was taken to apply to any type of meat, with the result that a 'rostbif' of lamb featured on more than one French menu. In the early nineteenth century an anglophile restaurateur cheerfully recommended to his customers such traditional English delicacies as *mach-potetesse* and *plumbuting*.

These aberrations apart, French writers were deeply engrossed in perfecting what they already regarded as the 'classic' cuisine, though whether a style of cooking which had been established for little over a century really warranted such a title is open to debate. In 1803 Grimod de la Reynière began publication of the *Almanac des Gourmands*, the original good food guide. He also set up a 'jury of tasters' who pronounced (not always impartially) on the virtues of dishes submitted by local tradesmen and innkeepers. In 1808 Grimod felt compelled to bring out his *Manuel des Amphitryons* (*Handbook for Hosts*) for the instruction of the *nouveaux riches*, who were not always as aware of the conventions and proprieties as they ought to have been. The art of cookery itself owes little to Grimod de la Reynière, but he certainly loosed the first puffs of that philosophic smokescreen behind which French gastronomes still wander today. Those philistines to whom a good meal brings bodily pleasure rather than spiritual revelation have little in common with Grimod and his heirs.

The early nineteenth century gave food not only a philosophic vocabulary,

53] A seventeenth-century 'still life' which might almost be a twentieth-century colour photograph. It has always been one of the greatest challenges to any artist (or photographer) to sum up the whole of a good meal in the ruins of its end. It is a challenge, and in this case a result, which Grimod de la Reynière would have approved

but a scientific one as well. The cookery books of the period are thick with jargon attempting to explain the chemistry of cookery. This was partly a result of the mental attitude induced by the industrial revolution and partly due to the influence of one very remarkable man—an American, Benjamin Thompson, who was knighted by George III and later nominated count of the Holy Roman Empire by the elector of Bavaria. Count Rumford, as he was generally known, became deeply concerned over the number of beggars in the Electorate and for some time devoted his attention to the problem of feeding the poor in a satisfactory manner for the least possible expenditure. He was convinced that water had nutritional value, and that barley was full of goodness, and bolstered his arguments with 'scientific' common sense. The obvious inference was that soup could provide maximum nourishment for minimum outlay. Barley soup thickened with potatoes and peas and seasoned with vinegar and salt was therefore served to the poor. Snippets of stale bread were incorporated in the soup, because Count Rumford's analytical eye had

54] In hot climates, where a large open fire for cooking would have been intolerable all the year round, earthenware stoves filled with charcoal were often used. Their usefulness diminished, however, as charcoal became scarce and expensive

observed that 'this hard and stale bread . . . renders mastication necessary, and mastication seems very powerfully to assist in promoting digestion. It likewise prolongs the duration of the enjoyment of eating, a matter of very great importance indeed.' The soup was designed to be wholesome and nourishing, but Count Rumford maintained that it was also 'very far from being un-palatable'. Including all ingredients (except for some of the bread, which local bakers willingly gave away because it was so stale) as well as wages for the kitchen staff, fuel, and a proportion of the annual write-off against repairs, Rumford was able to feed twelve hundred Munich poor for the total sum of £1 7s 6⅔d per day. Modern dieticians know that such a soup was by no means as nourishing as Rumford believed; but in his day the science of dietetics was scarcely even in its infancy. It was not unreasonable that he should equate a full stomach with sufficiency of nourishment—and, certainly, a stomach full of barley soup was preferable to a stomach full of nothing.

The most interesting outcome of Rumford's experiments, however, was in the field of fuel saving. Previously, most cooking had been done over large open fires which used a great deal of expensive fuel. This was an unsatisfactory and uneconomic system, especially when barley soup—which needed several hours' cooking—was involved. Count Rumford applied his considerable mind to the subject and ultimately produced a closed-top range which made ingenious use of almost all the heat of the fire, at the same time reducing the size of fire necessary. Flues, dampers and metal plates permitted the tempera-ture to be adjusted, and it was no longer necessary to fill the oven with hot coals which had to be raked out before cooking could proceed.

Rumford's writings had a wide circulation, and the kitchen range very soon came into general use. It caused a minor revolution in food and cookery, because now that heat could be controlled it became possible for food to be sautéed; fine sauces could be produced; and the new oven—unlike the old, which had faded relentlessly from hot to cool—made the soufflé possible. The French soon made the most of all the possibilities, and a new delicacy appeared in cooking, a delicacy which permitted such fragile foods as the truffle to appear in a new light. Truffles had been known in Roman times, though the Romans were none too sure of their origins. Pliny had argued that they were really balls of earth. 'We know for a fact that when Lartius Licinius, an official of praetorian rank, was serving as minister of justice at Cartagena in Spain a few years ago, he happened, when biting a truffle, to come on a denarius contained inside it which bent his front teeth; this will clearly show that truffles are lumps of earthy substance balled together.' In France the truffle had been forgotten during the Dark Ages, and when it was reintroduced in the fourteenth century the custom was to pickle it in vinegar, soak it in hot water, and then serve it in butter. The French chose to forget it once more until Catherine and Marie de Medici brought the Italian variety

55] Hunting for truffles, 1850. Pigs were usually used to root out these delicacies

with them in the sixteenth century. La Varenne, in the seventeenth century, had mixed truffles with mushrooms, but it was only in the nineteenth century that France really began to appreciate the true flavour of the fungus. Suddenly, truffles became very fashionable indeed. So much was written in their praise by poetic gastronomes that the demand trebled, and so did the price. The truffle never looked back, and it remains the one delicacy about which food writers universally wax lyrical.

Although society's upper crust benefited from these refinements, and although French chefs created a profitable aura of mystique around them, the nineteenth century was not without its difficulties. Many chefs who had served in aristocratic households before the revolution afterwards drifted into the restaurant business; when the restoration came, some of them returned to private service. But both noble households and fashionable restaurants were subject to the political upheavals which characterized France throughout the century. As emperors, kings and presidents came and went, so did the aristocracy. Revolutions killed fashions as well as people. It was not a happy time for chefs. Publishers of cookery books, however, were more adaptable—a simple change in the title enabled a book to survive all vicissitudes. In 1806, for example, A. Viard wrote *Le Cuisinier Impérial*. At the restoration it was retitled *Le Cuisinier Royal*. In 1848 Louis Napoleon was president of the republic, and Viard's book became known as *Le Cuisinier National*. But not

56] Nineteenth-century French chefs were much inclined to travel. The great Carême numbered among his employers British Prince Regent. In Carême's day, the Royal Pavilion kitchens were reconstructed by Nash (as in this picture)

for long; Louis Napoleon transformed himself into Napoleon III and in 1852 *Le Cuisinier National* hastily changed its name back to the *Impérial* of its early days. When the Third Republic was established in 1871, *Le Cuisinier* once more became—and remained—*National*.

In the middle of the nineteenth century, the poor in France were no better nourished than their contemporaries in England, and rarely had meat on their tables. Millions of Frenchmen, said the naturalist Isidore St Hilaire, ate no animal food, yet every year millions of pounds of excellent meat were wasted. He was talking about horsemeat, and claimed that even elderly work-horses made very good eating. In Paris, Toulouse and Berlin, horseflesh banquets suddenly became all the rage. In 1855 the director of the veterinary college at Alfort, M. Renault, had a twenty-three-year-old horse brought to him suffering from incurable paralysis. The horse was slaughtered and, three days later, eleven guests were invited by M. Renault to attend a 'comparative tasting'. Preparation and cooking had been strictly controlled, and each dish of horse was matched by a dish of finest beef. The tasters concluded that horse bouillon was superior to beef bouillon and that roast fillet of horse was better than roast fillet of beef. Boiled horse, though somewhat inferior to the finest boiled beef, was nevertheless much to be preferred to boiled beef of average quality.

Horsemeat became a perfectly acceptable food in France, but not in Britain, although attempts were made to introduce it in the 1860s. At a widely publicized dinner held in London in 1868, the menu included roast fillet of Pegasus, horse sausages with pistachio nuts, patties of Bucephalus-marrow, lobster with Rosinante-oil mayonnaise, and—with a descent to the commonplace—boiled withers. It must have been an interesting change from the average London dinner which Thackeray had complained of some years earlier. 'Everybody has the same dinner in London,' he said, 'and the same soup, and the same saddle of mutton, boiled fowls and tongues, entrées, champagne, and so forth. Who does not know those made dishes with the universal sauce to each: fricandeau, sweetbreads, damp, dumpy cutlets etc., seasoned with the compound of grease, onions, bad port wine, cayenne pepper, and curry powder?'

It was a sorry period in English cookery. Queen Victoria's chief cook, Charles Elmé Francatelli, published *The Modern Cook* in 1845, full of recipes for the inevitable turtle soup, for sheep's jowls, ears and trotters, as well as venison and reindeer's tongue. He was more concerned with tasteful presentation than tasteful food, with potatoes presented in fancy moulds and rice sculptured into appealing shapes (using a raw carrot as a chisel). In the same year, Eliza Acton produced *Modern Cookery for Private Families* where, in an attempt at international style, she perpetrated such atrocities as the 'King of Oude's Omlet', a kind of solid pancake loaded with leeks, mint and pepper. The great Alexis Soyer, chef of the Reform Club, was no more inspiring. Boiled neck of mutton and sheep's head were highlights of his *Shilling Cookery Book for the People*. Mrs Beeton, in 1861, offered a wide range of depressing recipes to the public; she did, however, make a very serious attempt to provide realistic estimates of costs, quantities and preparation times.

The cookery writers of the time might have argued that they were supplying what the public wanted—recipes for good, plain food. Unfortunately, though the food was certainly plain, it was all too rarely good. For many years, suppliers had increased their profits by adulterating the food they sold: bread was whitened with alum, cheese coloured with red lead, dried blackthorn leaves sold in place of tea, lead was added to cider and wine, and flour and chalk to milk. Complaints about such practices were not new, but the nineteenth century endorsed these complaints in the much-respected language of science. Frederick Accum successfully alienated every brewer in the land during the first decades of the century by naming not only the abuses but the abusers. In 1850 the *Lancet* took the matter up, energetically supported by *Punch*, which had a strong social conscience. Dr Hassall, a member of the *Lancet*'s Analytical and Sanitary Commission, made endless tests of offending products which were well publicized and began to have some effect on the

57] In London, milk could be bought straight from the cow—a pleasant thought. But the cows were ill fed and ill housed, and their milk was often the source of epidemics

authorities. For many a long day, however, the criminal ingenuity of small suppliers proved more than a match for the government's Food and Drugs Acts. It was only when massive manufacturing and retailing organizations began to appear that the small shopkeeper discovered that his business depended on his reputation. Condensed milk might not be better than good, fresh milk, but it was certainly better than the watered, germ-laden liquid sold in city dairies; margarine could not compete with good butter, but it was better and cheaper than the rancid butter which was all that many town tradesmen supplied; Smith's Patent Germ Bread might not sound very appetizing, but no one ever suggested that it was loaded with sand or alum. Small retailers had to have second thoughts when they were confronted with competition from such people as the redoubtable Tommy Lipton—who paraded gaunt and haggard men through the streets labelled 'Going to Lipton's', and fat and beaming successors labelled 'Coming from Lipton's'.

Just as the seventeenth century had seen the end of an era of new foods, it saw the beginning of an era of new drinks. It was reputedly Dom Pérignon who, at the abbey of Hautvilliers, first put the sparkle in Champagne. Cognac was evolved, too, in the Charente; the inhabitants had little sale for their white wine in its natural state, but found that when it was reduced by boiling (initially for the simple purpose of cutting transport costs) it became very popular indeed. The further discovery that a remarkable velvety quality could be achieved if the distilled wine were aged in casks of Limousin oak set the seal on Cognac's future. Port, formerly an innocuous table wine, acquired a new character in the early eighteenth century when the Oporto shippers discovered how to fortify and mature it.

In eighteenth-century England drinking reached such an extreme level that some observers seriously feared for the stability of the social structure. The poor lived in abominable conditions, particularly in the towns, and it seemed to many of them that no way of life could be worse than what they already suffered. 'British brandy', an extremely cheap, rough spirit made from malted corn or other materials, paid practically no excise duty; when it had been doctored with juniper it bore a passing resemblance to Dutch gin. It was so cheap that even the very poorest felt they could afford to drown their sorrows in it, and everyone conspired to help them do so. Although a licence was needed to sell beer, none was required for spirits, and it was estimated that, in certain quarters of London, one house in every four or five was a gin shop. Theft and violence, disease and death, were the inevitable results of addiction to a spirit that was too often made, not from malted grain, but from oil of

58] Hogarth's *Gin Lane*, a searing comment on London in 1751

turpentine, sulphuric acid, spirits of wine and lime water. Finally, in the middle of the eighteenth century, the authorities became seriously frightened and embarked on drastic measures to suppress an evil which their own lethargy had helped to create.

Of the three staple non-alcoholic drinks of the modern world—tea, coffee and chocolate—chocolate was the first to arrive in Europe. The conquistadors brought it back from the Americas to Spain, and it soon became known in the

59] An early London coffee-house

Spanish Low Countries. In 1631 Antonio Colmenero claimed that chocolate was very widely drunk indeed in Spain, Italy and Flanders. It had not, however, become popular elsewhere, and Colmenero's recipe may suggest several reasons why:

'For every hundred cacao beans, mix two berries of chilli or Mexican pepper —those large berries which are called *chilpatlague*—or, failing those, two Indian peppercorns, a handful of aniseed, two of those flowers known as 'little ears' or *vinacaxtlides*, and two of those known as *mesasuchil*. . . . Instead of the latter one could include the powder of the six roses of Alexandria [the 'six roses' used by apothecaries] . . . a little pod of logwood, two drachmae of cinnamon, a dozen almonds and as many hazelnuts, half a pound of sugar, and enough arnotto [a dye-plant] to give colour to the whole.'

Colmenero added that this particular chocolate recipe was intended for persons who enjoyed good health. The minor ingredients could be adapted to benefit sufferers from various ailments.

Although the Spaniards soon simplified the making of chocolate by adding only sugar or honey, and vanilla or cinnamon to the cacao beans, the drink still met with resistance elsewhere. It entered France, not as a pleasant drink, but as a medicine. This, however, was nothing unusual. Coffee and tea were both advertised in their early days in Europe for their health-giving rather than pleasurable qualities. In 1659 letters patent were granted to one David Chaliou allowing him the exclusive privilege of manufacturing and selling chocolate throughout France. His business must have flourished, helped by the faculty of medicine's approval of the drink in 1661. The court began to favour it, and all must have seemed well. But fashion proved inconstant as ever. A few years later, the marquise de Sévigné—who had been an early enthusiast—recorded that she had heard many unpleasant things about chocolate. 'The marquise de Coëtlogon took so much chocolate, being pregnant last year, that she was brought to bed of a little boy who was black as the devil!'

It was to be some time before chocolate was generally accepted in France, but in England, for a while at least, the rich preferred it to coffee—partly, no doubt, because it was more expensive. Coffee and chocolate were both introduced into the country at much the same time, and in the 1650s coffee-houses sprang up all over London. For some years, British and French travellers in the Middle East had spoken of the Turkish drink in the books they published when they returned from their wanderings. It may have been curiosity which first directed Londoners to the new coffee-houses, but it was the institution of the coffee-house itself which sent them back again and again. It was not entirely coincidence that made the coffee-house such a social centre. Men who had already heard of coffee—and they probably formed the majority of the first customers—were men of literary tastes, men who read travel books. They visited a new coffee-house and found that the other visitors were also men of literary tastes and men who read travel books. Nothing was more natural than that both the coffee and the company should grow to be a habit. In a very short time, certain groups gravitated towards certain coffee-houses, where they could be sure of meeting friends. Authors and writers foregathered at Will's, Whigs at the St James, Tories at the Cocoa Tree, financiers at Jonathan's. The history of the coffee-houses is a fascinating one—and there must be some significance in the fact that the coffee-house in England developed into the exclusive London club, whereas in France it became the open-to-all café.

Coffee, in France, had been credited with every medicinal property imaginable. It cleared humours from the brain, released wind, fortified the liver, refreshed the heart, relieved stomach disorders and lack of appetite. Its fumes were good for eye troubles and roaring in the ears, shortness of breath and lung congestion. It was also good for a hangover, and an unbeatable remedy for—shades of the Middle Ages—those who had eaten too much fruit. Nothing, it might be thought, had been left unsaid. What claims could the rival tea make in face of such competition? Apologists for tea did not blench for a moment. Tea, they said, was an infallible cure for migraine, drowsiness, apoplexy, lethargy, paralysis, vertigo, epilepsy, catarrh, colic, gallstones and consumption.

Tea had first been brought from China by the Dutch East India Company in the middle of the seventeenth century. It was, however, very expensive, hovering around the £4-per-lb mark for some years. The price did not reduce enough for it to become common in England until well into the eighteenth century, but by 1760 duty was being paid on five million lb of tea a year and it was estimated that almost as much was being smuggled in from France, duty free. While tea was comparatively rare, medical men did not greatly concern themselves over the advertisers' claims for it. But when the situation arose in which the great mass of the poor existed almost entirely on tea and bread, they began to take notice. It was not so much the tannin that worried them as the fact that tea was drunk hot and in large quantities, which they took to be very bad for the system.

It is not easy to understand why tea became the favourite drink of the British people. It cannot have been because it was filling; coffee and chocolate are far more satisfying drinks. It cannot have been because it was cheap; coffee and chocolate were both much cheaper. It cannot have been because people thought tea nourishing; doctors and politicians pointed out, frequently and vocally (and truthfully), that beer was far more nourishing.

Whatever the reason, tea did become Britain's national drink. In the north, it gave its name to a meal; in the south to a genteel social occasion. The English afternoon tea is unique, and the classic tea party of all time was not the Mad Hatter's, but an almost-normal one described by the artist Benjamin Robert Haydon which Mrs Siddons enlivened with readings from *Macbeth*:

'After her first reading the men retired to tea. Whilst we were all eating toast and tinkling cups and saucers, she began again. It was like the effect of a Mass bell at Madrid. All noise ceased; we slunk to our seats like boors, two or three of the most distinguished men of the day, with the very toast in their mouths, afraid to bite. It was curious to see Lawrence [Sir Thomas Lawrence, the portrait painter] in this predicament, to hear him bite by degrees, and then stop for fear of making too much crackle, his eyes full of water from the constraint; and at the same time to hear Mrs Siddons' "eye of newt and toe of frog!", and then to see Lawrence give a sly bite, and then looked awed and pretend to be listening.'

Haydon's own comment on the occasion was a model of restraint. 'I came away', he said, 'highly gratified.'

60] The sedate tea party of England was served by some of the most beautiful ships ever to sail the sea—the slim, elegant clippers, many of them American, which raced over the oceans of the world, sometimes carrying tea, sometimes grain, sometimes immigrants

Epilogue

It takes little imagination to visualize the tea party which Haydon described—
Mrs Siddons, majestic bosom swelling above the high waist of her dress; the
gentlemen tight-trousered, dark-coated, but by no means drab; the table set
with fine silver; the furniture decorated with Egyptian, Grecian or Gothick
motifs; the walls pale, the curtains richly swagged. Regency artists recorded
such costumes and interiors many times.

But artists, as recorders of the domestic scene, have had their ups and
downs during the centuries. For long periods, in fact, they scarcely recorded
it at all. This is hardly the place to go into the extremely complex history of
the *purpose* of art; but it must be said that, with only a few exceptions, what
we call 'art' was, in the early stages of most civilizations, strictly the servant of
religion and worship. When the gods were remote from humanity, art was
equally so. When the gods came down into the market place, art came with

61] Cézanne: 'Still Life'. An artist's vision in the nineteenth century

them. In Egypt, kings had certain attributes of divinity; their tombs and papyri show huntsmen and fishermen, bakers and banqueters, harvesters and herdsmen. In imperial Rome, where there were hero-gods and deified emperors, the murals, sculptures and mosaics illustrate the same wide range of human activity. In Buddhist India, temple sculpture represented the Buddha surrounded by the everyday life of the sculptors' own time. In Christian Europe, by contrast, it was to be many centuries before the daily pursuits of man intruded into the artists' vision of the Bible story. Nevertheless, with the conspicuous exception of the 'Dark Ages' in Europe and parallel periods on other continents, everyday life through the ages is comparatively well documented, particularly in the case of trades and occupations related to food.

The representation of food itself is quite another matter. Artists, in general, have been inclined to paint it in its natural rather than cooked state. There were two major reasons for this. Firstly, it was easier to identify—which most artists and patrons prior to the twentieth century regarded as a virtue. Secondly, it side-stepped the fact that food depends as much for its appeal on sense of smell as it does on sight, by showing the fresh colours and crisp shapes of raw materials, by offering the appetizing promise of food tomorrow rather than an aroma-less substitute for food today. The paintings by Pieter Aertsen (illustration no. 26) and Jan Davidsz de Heem (no. 49) illustrate this forcefully enough. So, too, does the Cézanne (no. 61). The delicate tints of his onions represent the best of art and of food; but it is doubtful whether even Cézanne could have given beauty to a dish of the pallid, cooked vegetable.

A serious attempt to paint cooked food was made only at a comparatively late stage in European art. This, it is fair to say, was almost as much the result of developments in cooking as of developments in art. Food in the Middle Ages was not beautiful to look at. Roasts apart—and some of the roast peacocks and swans in full plumage served at great tables were admittedly splendid—the dishes served consisted mainly of tidbits and of stews, sludgy in texture and either dull brown or saffron in colour. These offered no inspiration to the artist. Indeed, this problem was not unique to the Middle Ages; colour photographers today face the same problem when they are confronted with a *daube* or *carbonade*—and overcome it by studding the brown surface with uncooked, or separately cooked carrots, peppers and onions. Frequently, therefore, in mediaeval manuscripts and Renaissance paintings the only recognizable food is poultry or joints of meat (see illustration no. 30). Just as frequently, in banquet scenes, the diners' plates were shown empty or almost so (see the Veronese painting, no. 34). This may partly have been intended to suggest that the food had been good, but it also offered a simple solution to an awkward problem.

It was a problem which also, to some extent, confronted artists in China and India. Chinese painting, however, was either mistily impressionist or extremely detailed. The fine brushes of the painters could suggest every grain of sugar on a sweetmeat; the engraver was capable of delineating every grain of rice in a bowl. Indian painting, on the other hand, though of considerable delicacy at the height of the Mughal period, was more inclined to show the decoration on a dish than the food inside it. Later, during the British period, Indian artists turned towards the representation of trades—the spice seller, the arrack maker, the dairyman—but not to banquets or to still lives in the idiom of tenth-century China or seventeenth-century Europe.

In Europe, a change finally came about when art began to free itself first from courtly life and then from religion. Caravaggio brought realism, not only to the figures of the New Testament, but also to their surroundings and their food (see no. 35). Within a few decades, Dutch and Flemish artists in particular were deeply engrossed in a bourgeois world (a world, appositely enough, which had been enriched by the capture of the Spice Islands). The fine porcelain and silver, the solid possessions that were an index of prosperity, began to appear in paintings, their material worth emphasized by the casual way in which they were surrounded by rich foods (see, again, the De Heem still life, no. 49). The old antipathy to fruit and vegetables had faded, and the art of cooking had expanded. The kitchen had already become a favourite subject for wood engravings; soon it entered the painters' repertory.

Artists now also began to face the challenge of *prepared* food—even of food that was already half consumed. Willem Claesz Heda met the challenge superbly in his end-of-the-meal study of a remarkably luscious-looking pie (no. 53). Others were less successful. Chardin, in the following century, produced 'still lives' which enchant connoisseurs of art but fail to stimulate the gastric juices. French artists persevered with the theme of food, although the rococo world of the eighteenth century produced such dubious gastronomic sights as Oudry's painting of a dead and unplucked duck flanked by a ginger-studded cream pudding. In both France and England, cookery books were often delightfully illustrated. But in English painting, food became slightly suspect. Pictures of genteel dinner parties were by no means unknown, but the great age of the satirist had begun, and a favourite subject for caricature was food—or, to be more precise, the guzzling of large amounts of food.

The still life came into its own once more in the late nineteenth century,

62] Jeffrey: 'Still Life'. A photographer-artist's vision in the twentieth century

though in a much simplified form, when the Impressionists turned their attention to everyday living. But, for the time being, at least, this was virtually the end of food in art. As art has become more and more stylized, less and less representational, food—at least in a recognizable and appetizing form—has vanished from it. The soup tins and cereal packets which loom so large in Pop Art are no substitute. Good-looking, desirable, enticing pictures of food are now the province of the colour photographer, who is the real still-life artist of the mid-twentieth century. And, like his forebears, he still inclines towards, and succeeds best with, the raw materials of dining, the tantalising promise of wonderful food——tomorrow.

List of Illustrations

39] October. Wall-painting of the first half of the fifteenth century. *Castello del Buonconsiglio, Trento.*

40] Wine gauger. From the *Ordonnances de la Prévoste des Marchans et Eschevinaige de la Ville de Paris, 1415,* edition dated 1500. *Bibliothèque Nationale, Paris.*

41] Turkey. From the *Codex Mendoza* manuscript. *Bodleian Library, Oxford.*

42] Turkey. From Marx Rumpolt: *Ein New Kochbuch* (1604 edition). *By courtesy of the Trustees of the British Museum.*

43] Making tortillas. From the *Codex Mendoza. Bodleian Library, Oxford.*

44] Mexican Indians cultivating a walled garden. From the manuscript *Codex Osuna. Biblioteca Nacional, Madrid.*

45] Giuseppe Arcimboldo: 'Summer'. *Kunsthistorisches Museum, Vienna.*

46] 'How the savages roast their enemies'. From André Thevet: *La Cosmographie Universelle* (1575).

47] Wall panel from Moses Marcy House, Southbridge. *Photograph: Old Sturbridge Village regional museum, Massachusetts.*

48] Edward Hicks: 'The Cornell Farm'. *National Gallery of Art, Washington, D.C. Gift of Edgar William and Bernice Chrysler Garbisch.*

49] Jan Davidsz de Heem: 'Still Life'. *By courtesy of the Trustees of the Wallace Collection, London.*

50] Pierre Paul Sevin: 'The banquet which Clement IX gave to the queen of Sweden, at Monte Cavallo 1667' [in fact, 1668]. *Kungliga Biblioteket, Stockholm.*

51] Bonnard engraving, *c.* 1680, 'Vinegar merchant'.

52] Abraham Bosse: 'The pastry cooks', from a series of engravings of trades. *By courtesy of the Trustees of the British Museum.*

53] Willem Claesz Heda: 'Still Life'. *The Louvre, Paris.*

54] Diego Rodriguez de Silva Velazquez: 'An Old Woman cooking Eggs'. *By courtesy of the National Gallery of Scotland, Edinburgh.*

55] Engraving by Charles Emile Jacque, 1850, 'The truffle hunt'. *Bibliothèque Nationale, Paris.*

56] The kitchen of the Royal Pavilion, Brighton. From John Nash: *The Royal Pavilion at Brighton* (1827). *By courtesy of the Trustees of the British Museum.*

57] George Scharf the Elder: 'Golden Lane'. *By courtesy of the Trustees of the British Museum.*

58] William Hogarth: 'Gin Lane', engraving published 1 February 1751. *By courtesy of the Trustees of the British Museum.*

59] Anonymous watercolour, signed A.S. 1668, of a coffee-house. *By courtesy of the Trustees of the British Museum.*

60] Skillet: 'The clipper *Hurricane*'. *By courtesy of the Peabody Museum of Salem, Mass.*

61] Paul Cézanne: 'Still Life, onions and bottle'. *The Louvre, Paris.*

62] *Photograph by Jeffrey, Copyright* House and Garden.

Notes on Sources

Page 7 SYDNEY SMITH Letter 30 September 1837. *A Memoir of the Reverend Sydney Smith* by his daughter, Lady Holland, with *A Selection from his Letters* edited by Mrs Austin. 2 vols. 2nd edn 1855.

Page 7 UPANISHADS *Chandogya Upanishad* VII 9. Trs. F. Max-Müller. 1879–82.

Page 9 SUMERIAN INSCRIPTIONS Quoted in S. N. Kramer: *The Sumerians.* 1964.

Page 11 PLINY Pliny the Elder: *Natural History* XVIII 47. Trs. H. Rackham. 1950 edn.

Page 11 EGYPTIAN PAPYRUS Quoted in Isaac Meyer: *Oldest Books in the World.* 1900.

Page 12 ATHENAEUS Athenaeus: *The Deipnosophists* I 61. Trs. C. D. Yonge. 1854 edn.

Page 12 PAPYRUS OF BULAK As 'Egyptian papyrus', p. 11 above.

Page 12 CODEX MENDOZA *Codex Mendoza* fol. 70v. Trs. James Cooper Clark. 1938.

Page 14 ATHENAEUS I 62, see p. 12 above.

Page 15 ATHENAEUS I 60, see p. 12 above.

Page 16 HESIOD Hesiod: *Works and Days* 589–94. Trs. F. L. Lucas in *Greek Poetry for Everyman.* 1951.

Page 16 ILIAD Homer: *Iliad* XI and IX. Trs. E. V. Rieu. 1950.

Page 17 ATHENAEUS IV 15, see p. 12 above.

Page 18 TELECLIDES Quoted in Athenaeus VI 95, see p. 12 above.

Page 19 ARCHESTRATUS Quoted in Athenaeus I 7, see p. 12 above.

Page 19 HORACE (1 and 2) *Satires* II 8. Trs. H. Rushton Fairclough. 1926 edn.

Page 20 MARTIAL *Epigrams* X 48. 1904 edn.

Page 20 PETRONIUS Petronius: *The Satyricon* V 36 and 40. Trs. William Arrowsmith, 1960 edn.

Page 21 VITELLIUS Suetonius: *The Twelve Caesars* IX 13. Trs. Robert Graves. 1957 edn.

Page 22 PLINY XVIII 27, see p. 11 above.

Page 24 CHRYSIPPUS OF TYANA Quoted in Athenaeus XIV 57, see p. 12 above.

Page 24 PLINY XVIII 28, see p. 11 above.

Page 25 SUETONIUS Suetonius III 34, as 'Vitellius' p. 21 above.

Page 25 ALEXIS Quoted in Athenaeus II 44, see p. 12 above.

Page 26 CASSIODORUS Quoted in P. G. Molmenti: *Venice: The Middle Ages* I. 1906.

Page 28 CHARLEMAGNE Charlemagne: *De Villis*. Académie des Inscriptions et Belles-Lettres: *Mémoires* t. XXI. 1857.

Page 29 EGINHARD and MONK OF ST GALL. In *Early Lives of Charlemagne*, ed. A. J. Grant. 1907.

Page 30 PALLADIUS Palladius: *On Husbondrie* VIII 19 and XI 57, from an English manuscript *c.* 1420, ed. Rev. Barton Lodge. 1873.

Page 32 SALERNO REGIMEN Rhymed English version by Sir John Harington: *The Englishmans Doctor*. 1607.

Page 34 BHAGAVADGITA *Bhagavadgita* XVII 8–9. Trs. L. D. Barnett. 1905.

Page 34 MUHAMMAD Ibn Ishaq: *The Life of Muhammad*. Trs. Edward Rehatsek. 1964 edn.

Page 34 SALERNO See p. 32 above.

Page 34 DE JOINVILLE Quoted in Margaret Wade Labarge: *A Baronial Household of the Thirteenth Century*. 1965.

Page 41 ARTHASASTRA Kautilya: *Arthasastra* II 15.

Page 42 ARAB MERCHANT Quoted in *Rélation des Voyages . . . dans l'Inde et à la Chine dans le IXᵉ siècle*. Trs. M. Reinaud. 1845.

Page 44 SHE KING *She King* I xv I vi. Trs. James Legge. 1880

Page 46 SHE KING II vii VI iv, see p. 44 above.

Page 46 MARCO POLO *The Travels of Marco Polo*. Trs. Ronald Latham. 1968 edn.

Page 47 MARCO POLO See p. 46 above.

Page 47 ODORIC DE PORDENONE Quoted in *Cathay and the Way Thither*, ed. Sir Henry Yule. 1913.

Page 48 ODORIC See p. 47 above.

Page 50 HAJI MUHAMMAD As 'Odoric de Pordenone' p. 47 above.

Page 51 PETRARCH Petrarch: *Lettere Senili*. Quoted in Mrs Oliphant: *Makers of Venice*. 1905.

Page 52 GERMAN COMMISSION Quoted in E. Belfort Bax: *German Society at the Close of the Middle Ages*. 1894.

Page 55 MULLER As 'German Commission' p. 52 above.

Page 56 LUTHER *Wider die mordischen und Räubischen Rotten der Bauern*. 1525.

Page 56 POULTRY REGULATIONS City of London Archives 19 Edward III, Letterbook F fol. cii and ccii. Quoted in H. T. Riley: *Memorials of London*. 1868.

Page 57 JOHN, SON OF JOHN GYLESSONE 22 Edward III, Letterbook F fol. clii, as 'Poultry Regulations' p. 56 above.

Page 58 KILLERS OF SWINE 20 Edward I, Letterbook C fol. ii, as 'Poultry Regulations' p. 56 above.

Page 59 LONDON COOKSHOP William Fitzstephen: *Description of London*. Trs. H. E. Butler. 1934.

Page 59 COOKED MEAT PRICES 2 Richard II, Letterbook H fol. xcix, as 'Poultry Regulations' p. 56 above.

Page 59 VENETIAN AMBASSADOR Girolamo Lippomano, quoted in N. Tommaseo: *Rélations des ambassadeurs vénitiens*. 1838.

Page 60 GOODMAN OF PARIS *The Goodman* [Ménagier] *of Paris*. Trs. Eileen Power. 1928.

Page 61 LONDON SLAUGHTERHOUSES 43 Edward III, Letterbook G fol. ccxxxiii, as 'Poultry Regulations' p. 56 above.

Page 62 PARIS SLAUGHTERHOUSES Royal edict of August 1416. Quoted in Lespinasse: *Les Métiers et Corporations de la Ville de Paris*.

Page 63 GRAIN CHARACTERISTICS Henry Best: *Farming Book* (1641). 1857.

Page 63 DISHONEST BAKERS *Assisa Panis* (suppl.) fol. 79v, as 'Poultry Regulations' p. 56 above.

Page 67 BANQUET MENU *Opera di M. Bartolomeo Scappi*. 1570.

Page 70 BIRDS IN A PIE Epulario: *The Italian Banquet* (1516), English trs. 1598.

Page 70 FISH DAY BANQUET Cited in 'Devis et marchés passés par la ville de Paris pour l'entrée solennelle d'Elisabeth d'Autriche', in *Revue archéologique*. 1848–49.

Page 71 BODIN Quoted in M. L. Cimber and F. Danjou: *Archives curieuses*. 1834–40.

Page 73 NECKAM'S GARDEN Quoted in Sir Frank Crisp: *Mediaeval Gardens*. 1924.

Page 74 FLOWERS IN MEDICINE H. Lyte: *A Nievve Herball*. 1578.

Page 74 VENETIAN GARDENS Casola: *Viaggio*. 1494.

Page 75 CABBÁGES See 'Goodman of Paris', p. 60 above.

Page 76 RICHARD II'S SALAD *Forme of Cury*, publ. S. Pegge. 1780.

Page 77 FRA BONVICINO Fra Bonvicino da Riva: *The Fifty Courtesies for the Table* (*c.* 1290), trs. in *A Booke of Precedence*. 1869.

Page 77 THOMASIN Thomasin von Zerclaere: *The Italian Guest* (1215), trs. in *A Booke of Precedence*. 1869.

Page 78 TANNHÄUSER Tannhäuser: *Courtly Breeding*, trs. in *A Booke of Precedence*. 1869.

Page 78 DELLA CASA Giovanni della Casa: *Galateo* (*c.* 1550), trs. in *A Booke of Precedence*.

Page 78 FRA BONVICINO See p. 77 above.

Page 78 CELLINI Benvenuto Cellini: *Memoirs*. Trs. Miss Macdonell. 1907 edn.

Page 79 SIEUR DE VANDY Cited in Gédéon Tallemant, Sieur des Réaux: *Historiettes* (17th cent.). 1834.

Page 80 LE SAIGE *Chy sensuivent les gistes . . . [de] m. J.L.S.* 1520.

Page 82 DELLA CASA See p. 78 above.

Page 83 GOODMAN OF PARIS See p. 60 above.

Page 83 HIPPOCRAS *Nouvelle instruction pour les confitures et les liqueurs.* 1715 edn.

Page 85 SIR HUGH PLATT Sir Hugh Platt: *The Jewell House of Art and Nature.* 1594.

Page 86 COLUMBUS *The Life of the Admiral Christopher Columbus*, by his son Ferdinand (*c.* 1535). 1960 edn.

Page 86 FERDINAND As 'Columbus' above.

Page 87 DIAZ DEL CASTILLO Bernal Diaz del Castillo: *The True History of the Conquest of New Spain.* Trs. A. P. Maudsley. 1908–16.

Page 92 DIDEROT *Encyclopédie.* 1751–72.

Page 92 WINSLOW Edward Winslow: *Good News from New England.* 1624.

Page 93 STRACHEY William Strachey: *Historie of Travell into Virginia Britania.* 1612.

Page 94 MARKHAM Gervase Markham: *The English House-wife.* 1615.

Page 98 MRS MANN Mrs Horace Mann: *Christianity in the Kitchen.* 1861.

Page 100 DE HEEM Cited in J. von Sandrart: *Teutsche Academie.* 1675–79.

Page 102 LITHGOW William Lithgow: *The Totall Discourse.* 1632.

Page 103 VEGETABLES IN ENGLAND M. Misson's *Memoirs and Observations in his Travels over England.* Trs. Mr Ozell. 1719.

Page 104 MARIN François Marin: *Les Dons de Comus.* 1739.

Page 106 LAMB *Royal Cookery.* 1710.

Page 106 SARAH PHILLIPS *Ladies Handmaid.* 1758.

Page 106 ELIZA SMITH *The Compleat Housewife.* 1727.

Page 109 RUMFORD Count Rumford: *Of Food; and particularly of feeding the Poor.* 1795.

Page 110 RUMFORD See p. 109 above.

Page 110 PLINY XIX 11, see p. 11 above.

Page 113 THACKERAY W. M. Thackeray: *Memorials of Gourmandising.* 1845.

Page 117 COLMENERO *Tratado de la naturaleza y calida del chocolate.* 1631.

Page 118 DE SÉVIGNÉ Letter 25 October 1671. *Lettres de Mme de Sévigné.* 1862–75.

Page 119 HAYDON Benjamin Robert Haydon: *Correspondence and Table Talk.* 1876.